CRITICAL ISSUES IN EDUCATING AFRICAN AMERICAN YOUTH
(A Talk With Jawanza)

by Jawanza Kunjufu

AFRICAN AMERICAN IMAGES
Chicago, Illinois

Photographs by Henry Cheatham

First Edition
First Printing

Copyright ©1989 by Jawanza Kunjufu

Table of Contents

INTRODUCTION

I have been a local consultant since 1974 and a national consultant since 1977, on issues related to the education of Black youth. One of the things I've been very concerned with over the years is best characterized by a theoretical paradigm developed by Barbara Sizemore: You first establish what the problems are, then you ask yourself what caused the problems, and then you look at solutions for those problems, and lastly, you determine the implementation of those solutions. We seem to spend a lot more time in the first stage, the problem stage, which reminds me a great deal of what happens when the media glorify the negative, but rarely look at: (1) what caused those problems, (2) what are some of the solutions to those problems, and (3) the implementation of those solutions.

I would like a lot more attention to be given to what caused the problem, and even more given to the solution and implementation. However, besides the limited amount of time provided for a workshop, unfortunately the coordinators want the consultant or presenter to do the majority of the talking; and yet I think a lot of the answers and information that we need to secure exist within the audience. While it is a problem having a workshop where you immediately go to the questions because they can sometimes take you away from the central issues, it does require questions to be somewhat related and/or the coordinator or speaker to steer the questions in a centralized manner. I do think that students and teachers have been talked to enough, and now it's time for us to listen to each other and then have the kind of guided dialogue that I think would be more effective.

This book, then, is a collection of the most challenging questions that I've received since 1974 on issues related to the education of Black youth. The questions are categorized as they relate to: teachers and pedagogy, curriculum, learning styles, special education, Black boys, self-esteem, motivation, educational administration, parenting, and community involvement. Hopefully, you'll see your own questions throughout this book and its format will allow you to go directly to those areas and questions that interest you most. This way I think everyone is satisfied and you're receiving information that is directly pertinent to your concerns.

TO GOD BE THE GLORY

TEACHERS

Q: What is the most important factor impacting academic achievement?

A: There are a number of areas that impact the education of our children. I believe that teacher expectations, tracking, parental involvement, student self-esteem, curriculum, learning styles, test bias, and peer pressure are the major factors.

Areas that I feel are less significant are socio-economic factors related to the home environment, a student's innate ability, and per pupil expenditures. There are many teachers who believe the reason why children do not learn lies in the social demographics of the home. That is, if there are no fathers in the home, if the family's income is low, if the children speak Black English, or if the children are "culturally deprived," then the children will not learn. Later on we'll examine the research from Ron Edmonds and Reginald Clark which refutes the notion that children do not learn based on the "broken home" concept. I am not naive enough to believe that income is not a factor, but I like research that shows children can learn regardless of the number of parent or how much money is in the home.

Many teachers also believe that the reasons for the academic performance gap between White and Black students lie in ability; we don't believe that. When you look at the contrasting fact that 86% of the NBA's starters are Black but only 2% of today's engineers are Black, we don't believe that's attributed to ability; we believe that's attributed to the amount of time used for studying and the role models that our children see. If you ask young Black males to name five Black male athletes or five Black male entertainers, there's no problem, but when you ask them to name five Black men with college degrees, they have a great degree of difficulty. Recent SAT scores show that the average Asian American student is scoring 920, while the average European American student is scoring 908 and the average African American student is only scoring 720—but it's not because of ability. The average Asian American youth studies twelve hours a week; the average White student studies eight hours a week, and our youth only study five hours a week and watch more TV than anybody else in America.

We don't believe in the broken home argument, the ability argument, nor do we believe in the per pupil expenditure argument. These arguments are proposed by people who believe that you measure schools by the color of the school bus, or by how modern the gymnasium is. I'm from the old school: Tuscaloosa, Alabama, 1910, one-room school shack, forty students, a leaky roof, only two books, and all forty students learned. You shouldn't measure a school by the thickness of its carpet. You shouldn't measure a school by who a child sits next to. You should measure a school mainly by teacher expectations, and I believe that is *the* most important factor impacting academic achievement.

While I feel that teacher expectations are the most important factor, parental involvement is the second most important factor, followed by student self-esteem, curriculum quality, learning styles, test bias, and peer pressure. Throughout this book, we'll elaborate on some of these issues in more detail.

Q: Why is it difficult for some teachers to have high expectations of Black youth?

A: Research from Wilbur Brookover, who is also involved in the Effective Schools project, noted that some teachers lower their expectations based on the race of the child, the income of the child, the gender of the child, and the child's appearance. If the most important factor influencing academic achievement is teacher expectations, we cannot allow teachers to lower their expectations based on race, income, gender, or appearance.

Q: If we accept the premise that teacher expectations are the most important factor impacting academic achievement, how do we raise teachers' expectations of Black student achievement?

A: That's a very difficult question because it relates more to attitude than to information. Unfortunately, there's not a lot you can do with a teacher who has a bad attitude and does not believe that our children can learn. Interestingly, students know when they have a good teacher and when they have a bad teacher. The staff knows who's a good teacher and who isn't; and of course, the administrators also know. And yet, unfortunately, a child still attends a whole year of school with that unprepared teacher. I guess the attitude seems to be, "Well, it was only one year." And it's disappointing that we have allowed ourselves to reach this stage. Nevertheless, from the informational vantage point, there's an awful lot of research being developed showing the relationship between teacher expectations and academic achievement.

I'm a strong supporter of a program called TESA (Teacher Expectation Student Achievement). The theory says that if you increase teacher expectations, you'll increase academic achievement. The program combines in-service training with research materials. For a teacher who wants to learn the relationship between expectations and academic achievement, there's some very effective material available. But the problem, I think, lies moreso in a teacher's attitude. I sincerely believe that you have to love your students, you have to respect them and you have to understand their culture. There are many teachers, though, who do not love, respect, or understand African American culture; last but not least, they are afraid of our boys.

We have teachers who are racist; we have teachers who are sexist; we have teachers who do not bond with students of different economic or social strata. And so, those factors then impact academic achievement. We have to have strong administrators who will hold poor teachers accountable and make it uncomfortable for them to stay in classrooms. We have to have parents who, when their children tell them they have a poor teacher, recognize that it is unacceptable. And we have to begin to have teachers police themselves and hold themselves accountable.

Q: You mentioned the TESA program. What exactly is TESA? And why do you think it can be effective in the education of Black youth?

A: It is a research model looking at three major areas: response opportunities, feedback and reinforcement, and personal regard. Some school districts have trained some of their administrators or even have sent large portions of their staff to be trained in TESA. Initially, an administrator or someone on a school's staff will use a video camera to begin to observe a teacher's behavior in the classroom. The observer then writes comments related to expectations (for example, what was perceived from students' behavior, whether the teacher's behavior was conducive to maximizing a student's academic achievement, etc.).

One of TESA's concerns is that if you ask teachers whether they believe that our children can learn, the majority of them will say yes, even if they don't believe it. If you ask them if they have high expectations of students' achievement, they will again say yes. So TESA has attempted to break this generic response pattern down and begin to use some very specific, measurable evaluations of teachers' expectations. One example is response opportunities. TESA believes that children learn best when they're involved in the process of learning.

If we had to monitor a class (either with an administrator, a teacher, a video camera, or a tally sheet), would we see that all thirty children were given the same number of opportunities to respond? That's very difficult to do, even for the better teachers: to spread out the opportunities in such a way that all thirty children are involved in classroom discussions. Many teachers say that the reason why they don't call on "Willie" (a lower achiever), is because time is so precious, and they can't waste time calling on a student that does not know the answer. Well, that to me is quite a band-aid approach; when you stop calling on Willie in September or October, and then you decide to call on him in April, May or June, he will be even less likely to know the answer. So, good teachers have been able to figure out a way to have thirty children involved in classroom discussions.

The second area of the TESA program is feedback and reinforcement. TESA believes that children learn best when they're supported and encouraged, when there are clues given to them about the correct answers to questions, and when they're involved in classroom discussions. If we went into your classroom, would we see that you give the same amount of time, attention, reinforcement, and praise to all of your students? Or would we see that there are some students that are given a lot more praise, reinforcement, and feedback than others? For example, say you have two students named Willie (the lower achiever), and Ann (the higher achiever). If you ask Willie a question and Willie gets it wrong, would you stay with Willie for a few moments and begin to help him by giving him some clues so he can come up with the appropriate answer? Or would you — as the research has found — give approximately six seconds to your lower achievers (especially Black male students like Willie), but when Ann, the higher achiever, gets the answer wrong, provide almost three to four minutes to help the child answer the question correctly? I believe that Willie would answer the question correctly if he'd been given three to four minutes worth of clues as well.

The third large area of TESA's focus is the only one that cannot be taught, "personal regard." We need to begin to look at where children sit in the classroom, and why they sit in certain areas. We need to look at where teachers stand in the classroom. In many cases, there's something very interesting and significant about where children sit and teachers stand. Many teachers are not comfortable standing near certain students. TESA believes you have to love them. You have to be involved in their lives. Unfortunately, many teachers do not love our children. On occasion, I have had to counsel many a student who complains, "Ms. So-and-So does not like me." We attempt to explain to them that the teacher has vital information they need and there will be times when teachers will not like students. Black children, though, are extremely humanistic and find it hard to comprehend or appreciate that a teacher does not love them. TESA is an attempt to encourage teachers to show more concern.

Q: How do schools reflect the values of the dominant culture?

A: Schools teach our children more than the "Three R's." They also teach our children values. We used to value "We," but now many of us value "I." We used to value cooperation, but now many of us value competition. We used to value what we felt on the inside, but now we value what we see on the outside. There is an obvious promotion of "I, competition," and "external" in our society versus "We, cooperation," and "internal."

An example of how American schools reinforce "I-ness," competition, external goods, and elitism involves test scores. One child receives a score of 100 and another child receives a score of 40. In a typical American situation, the child with the 100 feels better than the one that received the 40. The child with the score of 40 has felt a lowering of his self-esteem, and there's some degree of tension between the two students. Sometimes, there's also a sense of arrogance and condescension from the student with the highest grade. And in some cases, the student with the high grade is teased by his peer group. But if different values are taught—a sense of "We-ness," cooperation, and appreciation for the inner self—the child that received 100 would be encouraged to help the child that received the score of 40.

Secondly, this kind of situation continues among adults. People with college degree(s) become very arrogant and condescending toward those without a college education. The communities where Black youth reside need the resources and expertise which college graduates have to offer, but because college graduates are not taught to bring their resources back, communities rarely receive the benefits of an accomplished student.

Schools obviously teach more than the "Three R's." They reinforce an ideology that civilization began with European culture, that you were not discovered until White people discovered you. Schools give a view of the world through the eyes and opinions of "founding fathers" like George Washington and Thomas Jefferson, who—from an African frame of reference—were slave owners. History remains "His-story." Unfortunately, we see the world not only through White eyes, but also white images. Schools reinforce that value system—they reinforce the red, white, and blue. And yet when we examine the Berlin Conference of 1880, when Europeans divided up Africa so they could further their colonization efforts, that event should not be viewed as White people bringing civilization to the African continent. Instead, Europeans brought imperialism and colonization to Africa. Schools therefore have been a social agent to promote the

6

interests of White America.

Q: How do you feel about tracking?

A: In my opinion, tracking does not work. Tracking reinforces America's value system in regard to elitism and helps to increase a widening gap between the "haves" and the "have nots." In the United States, only 4% of the people own 60% of the wealth. Our school system mirrors our economy. Tracking does not work. But you don't have to believe me, you can read John Goodlad's book, *A Place Called School*, and Ray Rist's study, published in the August, 1970 issue of *Harvard Educational Review*. Both of them point out that tracking does not work. Tracking insures that those in the lowest track will never catch up with those in the highest track, which might have been its original intention. America never said all children would be educated, it has never been said nor will it be said. Through methods like tracking, we play games with our children called advanced placement, honors, regular, basic, gifted and talented, special education, and magnet schools. These kinds of divisions reinforce the American economy, in which those that have will continue to have and those that do not have will continue to go without.

So those in the lowest track never catch up and the gap widens over time. I am very sensitive to teachers in fourth or fifth grade classrooms of thirty children, all with a wide array of abilities. This gap did not start in the fourth or fifth grade, it started as early as the eighth day of kindergarten, as Ray Rist points out in his research. But before we look in more detail at his study, let me reemphasize that those in the lowest tracks hardly ever catch up with those in the highest levels. In addition, those in the lowest tracks receive the poorest teachers and the least amount of resources. So, if you must divide children by ability, which educators are on record as saying tracking is not the most effective way to teach, you should at least make sure you give them the more advanced teachers and resources. Unless, as some have speculated, you never intended to close the gap. That may be the reason why those in the highest levels receive "master teachers" — the most experienced instructors — and the greatest amount of resources.

Ray Rist's study points out that as early as the eighth day of kindergarten—a long time before we play additional games like advanced placement, honors, basic, gifted and talented, and so on —teachers make permanent decisions about who is going to be in the highest, middle, and lowest groups of students. And yet, how much academic information can a teacher possibly have about a child on the eighth day of kindergarten? You're correct, they have very little, which means they then rely on the parental registration form, the social worker's interview, and how the child dresses. Children that do not dress neatly, do not sit among those in the highest group, do not smell well, speak Black English, do not have a father living in their home, and are not verbal with authority figures, are not placed with the highest group.

Now before I continue, I want to mention that many of you may be wondering if we can educate low income African American children. But that may not be the central question. The real question may be: Do middle income teachers want to teach children who come from low income families and are African American? For those that are now beginning to see the picture I am trying to create here, Rist found in his study that teachers chose children for the highest group who looked like their children: they dressed neatly, were well-groomed, smelled nice, spoke standard English, were verbal with adults, had fathers living in their homes, and were from middle income families. THEY CHOSE CHILDREN THAT LOOKED LIKE THEIR CHILDREN.

This was a longitudinal study. It did not stop on the eighth day of kindergarten, it also observed first and second graders. Those same children who as early as the eighth day of kindergarten were placed in the highest group, remained in the highest group during first and second grades. The children in the middle and lower groups also remained in their respective groups. The decision that was made on the eighth day of kindergarten became a permanent decision. So naturally when these children then enter the third through seventh grades, a large discrepancy exists among students.

The study goes on to say that those children in the lowest group received the lowest level of expectations, and those in the higher groups received higher expectations. It then becomes a self-fulfilling prophecy that those children in the highest group will be more advanced because they received the highest level of expectations. Those in the lowest group will be less accomplished because they did not receive the same high level of expectations. Teachers who advocate tracking give me some resistance to my viewpoint. Yes, there are going to be some recognizable differences in ability, especially when children reach the upper grades. But there are also differences in abilities because of some decisions that were made on the eighth day of kindergarten.

I would rather divide children (if we must divide them) into cooperative-learning, heterogeneous groups. Students that are higher, middle, and lower achievers will each be represented on any given team or group. (We will elaborate about cooperative learning when those questions arise.) I would also recommend that we divide children into groups by learning styles. I do not recommend dividing children by ability. I would prefer cooperative learning or learning styles as a method of organizing a classroom.

Q: How significant is family income and the number of parents in the home to academic achievement?

A: There have been numerous studies done by universities and school districts, looking at the variables of income and the number of parents in the home as they relate to academic achievement. In most cities, because of the neighborhood school concept, those students living in more affluent neighborhoods or school districts score higher on achievement tests. The disparity between suburban and inner-city schools appears to be a result of different income levels. A gap also exists between African American children attending suburban schools and those attending inner-city schools. Therefore, a variance in academic achievement appears to occur racially and economically.

But this is a very complex point for a number of reasons. First, you have to examine the motive of the research. I don't accept the notion of objectivity in research. I think that all research is subjective in some way. Researchers begin their studies looking for certain things; there's some kind of premise or hypothesis brought to the research. So, for instance, if a researcher finds that children learn better when there is a father in the home and the family has a median income of $30,000, what will that tell us? What are the implications of research like that? Do you think this researcher will make it easier for Black men and other men to stay home with their children? With findings such as these, if it has not already done so, do you think the federal government will then legislate an increase in benefits and wages? I find it very interesting that this kind of research is emerging just when people are struggling to convince Congress to substantially increase the minimum wage. We're not talking about the teenager working for $3.35 an hour, but the major bread winner. I really wonder about the motive of this kind of research.

Secondly, if we prove that those two variables are significant to academic achievement, what are the implications? Are we going to do anything with that information? Unfortunately, after seeing this kind of research teachers then throw up their hands and say, "See, what can I do?" Document after document point out that income and number of parents in the home determine academic achievement. Consequently, too many teachers are let off the hook. I think better research comes from people like Ron Edmonds and Reginald Clark who show that regardless of income and single- or two-parent homes, we can produce high-achieving students. Later we'll look at questions from the administrative perspective, and Ron Edmond's research on "effective schools." He looked at schools with students from low income families, studied which ones worked, and summarized their common features. I like that kind of research because it shows that in spite of the income level we can make a difference. I'm elated with research coming from Reginald Clark, and we'll look at his study on parents when we answer questions from the parental perspective. I'm pleased with research that shows it does not matter how many parents are in the home or how much money is earned, it boils down to the quality of the interaction between teacher and student. I'm not naive. I'm not trying to sell poverty. I'm not trying to ignore how significant income or having two parents in the home is. I'm on record in my best seller, *Countering the Conspiracy to Destroy Black Boys*, as saying that Black boys need Black male role models. But I also like research that shows schools with low income students and single female parents can produce high-achieving students.

Q: Why is there a disparity even with income being constant between Black and White students?

A: I'm a consultant nationwide with a program that is trying to close the achievement gap between Black and White students. On the national Iowa and California achievement tests, the average European American child is scoring in the 60th percentile and the average African American child is scoring in the 30th percentile on the same tests. I've also been a consultant to several middle income school districts such as Evanston, Illinois, Columbia, Maryland, and Cleveland Heights, Ohio. In those locations, the gap also persisted even though there was more of a homogeneously middle income population. In these middle income neighborhoods, the average White child scored in the 80th-85th percentile on the Iowa or California tests. The average Black child scored in the 50th percentile. While those school districts had African American students who scored higher than the norm for their racial group, a 30- to 35-point variance remained between the average Black and White child. That's what your question is reinforcing. Please note that whether we're talking about a low income or a middle income school, there are still teachers with low expectations for African American students.

Research shows that some teachers lower their expectations based on a student's race, income (although in this case that is not a factor), gender, and appearance. I think it would be fair to say that race is one factor that is influencing some of these teachers' expectations of Black students' academic performance. Please note that even in these middle income and so-called integrated schools, they may look integrated on the outside, but because of tracking, they are highly segregated on the inside. Ninety per cent of the advanced placement and honors classes are populated by White students, there's a racially integrated division of regular classes, and almost 90% of the lower or basic track consists of Black students. Many parents are not aware of what's going on inside these schools.

The disparity is also evident when we realize that the curriculum is Eurocentric. Whether we're talking about low or middle income students, Hippocrates, Columbus, Washington, and Lincoln are still the "Great White Fathers." In almost every case, schools reinforce a European-based value system. Later on, we'll discuss curriculum in more detail. Please also remember, though, that tests are culturally biased too. Any discussion of academic achievement really revolves around achievement tests and many of the questions on these tests are still culturally biased toward European history and culture. Holding the variable of income constant does not negate the fact that achievement tests are culturally biased in favor of European values and with little or no attention given to African-American values and culture. We really have to be much more sensitive to the impact of being a Black child in a White world, at a White school with White curriculum.

Q: My follow-up question, then, is if race, number of parents, neighborhood and income are not factors and then we held income constant and still saw a gap between Black and White students, what explains the success of Asian over Black students and even over White students in many cases? If the tests are culturally biased toward Europeans, what explains the success of Asian students on these tests?

A: That's a very complex question and one that we need to dissect to better understand this phenomenon. Recent SAT scores show that Asian-American students on average score 920, while the average White student scores 12 points lower and the average Black student scores 200 points lower.

This scoring gap is the result of numerous reasons. The average Asian-American youth studies 12 hours a week, four hours more than the average White student and seven hours more than the average Black student—who also watches more television than anyone else in the United States. Another reason for their scholastic success is hard work, the same ingredient you can attribute to our success in sports and music. Asian parents, because of their culture, revere academic achievement. In addition, the learning style of Asian-American students is conducive to American classrooms; they highly respect authority, discipline, and being studious and quiet at school. These are all traits that teachers admire and reward, in contrast to those of many Black students who in many cases are not as respectful, disciplined, studious and quiet as they should be. A lot of activity, noise, and other distractions are evident in many African-American homes and that kind of atmosphere limits academic achievement. Furthermore, many Black parents do not teach their children to respect authority figures as we once did. All these ingredients facilitate Asian-

American students' academic achievement, in contrast to what makes our own youths' achievement more fragile.

A closer examination of SAT scores reveals that Asian Americans outscore Whites on the math section, yet Whites outscore Asian-Americans on the verbal section of the test. That's understandable given Asian-American students' tendency to be much less verbal than their White counterparts. In some cases, there is even greater dependence on non-verbal interaction in the classroom if these students are recent immigrants to this country. Why, then, don't Black students outscore Asian-Americans on the verbal section of the SAT? The answer probably lies in our tendency to be verbal only as it relates to communication amongst ourselves and not in terms of classroom interaction based on standard English. In addition, many teachers give Asian-American students higher expectations than those they give African-American students. Even among Black students themselves, the assumption persists that any Asian-American students at their school will be the better students.

I'll never forget that when I was in high school—with a 95% Black majority—there was a student named Gordon Fujimoto. I refused to allow this student to outscore me in school. I was determined that, in a school with only 5% White and Asian population, I would not let them outperform me. We must have more competitive pride in the area of academic achievement. We need to use the same kind of confidence and pride used in athletics. So, the Black community must: 1) increase students' study time, 2) make learning the highest priority in our household, 3) create more quiet time at home, 4) demand more discipline from our youth, 5) have students respect authority, and 6) reinforce academic achievement in our community and culture.

Q: What are your views about abolishing social promotion and instituting minimal standards for advancement?

A: This trend is designed to regain trust from the public and specifically the taxpayers. Our society has grown concerned about students in high school who are reading on a third grade level. However, many teachers have expressed anguish at this policy, because they are not being given additional resources to address it. The burden of this decision, which is similar to Propositions 48 and 42 in college athletics, rests squarely on the students. This kind of policy does not require schools to increase teachers' expectations, better understand and deal with learning styles, or make the curriculum more relevant—all factors noted to be very effective ways to improve academic achievement. Studies have shown that where this mandate is in effect, dropout rates have increased, along with special education placements. These results were not the desired ends of this movement. I am in favor of standards, but not only those applied to students. Schools should be given additional resources, reduce classroom size, increase in-service training, and implement strategies to improve expectations, curriculum, etc.

Q: How can schools make up for the experiential background that many African American children lack when they come to school?

A: Your question indicates some positive assumptions. For instance, since schools in the United States are culturally biased toward the European American way of life, they operate from the perspective that children will bring to the classroom a frame of reference and experiences upon which they will build as they increase their knowledge. We know, especially among African American children, this is often not the case.

If a child has been to museums, the state capitol, or the White House, and has been able to see these places firsthand, then when he or she reads about them in school, a bond is created between theory and practice and there's a greater interest in learning. My own trip to Egypt, for example, enhanced my knowledge or Africa. When I think of the pyramids, that part of our history now means something totally different to me than had I not been there.

On the other hand, field trips and textbooks can be unproductive. When I visited the museum in Cairo, Egypt, it held some very significant objects, but the curator didn't design the exhibits so people could really understand what was displayed. Curators too often design exhibits like closets, filled with artifacts but lacking a central focus. Our children go on field trips to places like museums and don't fully comprehend what's being conveyed.

Many experiences that our children have are not respected and valued in the classroom. Consequently, there's no integration of curriculum with children's own experiences. The most compelling example of this gap is when our children are labeled "culturally deprived." Everyone has a culture. It may not be the teacher's culture, but everyone has a culture. When an adult labels a child "culturally deprived," it shows the adult's own arrogance and that he or she only respects people of cultures identical or similar to his or her own. When that happens, our children are deprived of opportunities to use their own experiences to make important links between their own world and the one introduced at school.

I think teachers' first step should be to review the achievement tests they administer and look for the cultural bias in the tests. Secondly, they should examine their curriculum to see how they can integrate their lesson plans with the tests. Many school districts offer a curriculum that does not expose children to all the information presented in standardized tests. In addition, many African-American youth attend schools with somewhat weak course requirements. They may not be required to take two to four years of high school math or science, or the school may not even offer physics, trigonometry, or other college preparatory courses. Yet recent studies show a direct correlation between high SAT/ACT scores and a college preparatory curriculum. Every effort should be made to secure encyclopedias and other resource materials for our children. The American school system assumes that every child will have these resources. Securing funding for these materials should not be viewed as naive or idealistic. After all, in 1988 the Chicago public schools bought calculators for all its students. Lastly, students' own experiential make-up should not be ignored or depreciated. Once teachers use all these suggestions, they should find that they can more than make up for any experiential differences among their students.

Q: In the "Effective Schools" research, a number of correlates were offered by Ron Edmonds. One of these was "time on task." How can we improve and increase "time on task"?

A: "Time on task" is a very significant factor of academic achievement. It is erroneous to assume that every public school student in this country will receive the same number of instructional hours, even within the same school. There are teachers who spend a lot of time disciplining students and attending to administrative tasks and other interruptions that reduce the amount of time they spend on the task of teaching. During a typical 9:00 a.m. to 3:00 p.m. school day, even 15 uninterrupted minutes daily can be critical; 15 minutes a day multiplied by 5 weekdays is 75 minutes, and 75 minutes multiplied by a 40-week school year equals 3 whole weeks of instructional time. Do you know what a good teacher can do with three whole weeks of instruction? Do you know how much you pay a tutor by the hour?

One of the factors affecting time on task and which needs correcting is discipline. In many classrooms, teachers have to spend time telling children to sit down, be quiet, etc. That is not instructional time. One of the ways, therefore, to increase time on task is to have a more disciplined class. A little later we'll discuss disciplinary strategies. If we can improve classroom discipline we will in itself increase instructional time.

Another distractor to time on task involves administrative issues, especially with grade levels — like those in junior and senior high — where students change classrooms during the school day. Research has shown that in many cases the first eight minutes and the last nine minutes of a 50-minute period are lost with some kind of administrative duties. A total of 17 minutes is often wasted, leaving only 33 minutes for instruction. One way to avoid some of that waste is for the teacher to have instructional material ready to present (on the chalkboard or as a hand-out) when students arrive. Then the students can immediately begin working while the teacher takes attendance or performs some other administrative task. Of course, some principals, secretaries or other staff see no problem with interrupting instructional time with lunch forms, field trip slips, announcements and other distractions. While this is an unfortunate part of any school day, it should not be given a high priority. In high achieving schools there is regular, mandatory quiet time for reading and instruction.

Another area influencing time on task concerns the division within a classroom into groups. Let's say there's a typical elementary class divided into three or four ability groups. If you observe the class, you'll likely find the teacher presenting instruction to one group while disciplining another group. Instructional time is not occurring in this situation. This is not just a disciplinary problem, it also relates to management strategies and ability group-ings. A better disciplined class and cooperative learning groups could increase instructional time.

The last aspect of time on task is attitude. In-service training can be useful, but there are still lazy teachers. Some teachers simply have a stronger work ethic than others. We need principals who will mandate greater productivity.

Q: How can we increase the number of Black teachers, especially African-American male teachers?

A: With the onset of integration, we have lost over 31,000 teachers. Many Black principals at Black schools became teachers and teachers lost their jobs. There are a number of ways to look at the decline of African-American teachers. Presently we're 8% of the public school staff and that is expected to drop to 5% by the year 2000, while simultaneously we're 17% of public school students, a figure that's expected to rise to 25% by 2000. As you can see, a continuing problem definitely exists.

Some positive aspects also exist. Historically, because of institu-tional racism, Black college-graduates were limited to a few fields of employment, including teaching. Many of our best Black minds were all in the education industry. We had people who could have become engineers, mathematicians, lawyers, or other professionals, but they were unable to because of institutional racism. The good news about this part of our history meant that many of our former teachers were outstanding in a particular sub-ject area and were able to pass on their knowledge and interest in a field they ironically could not enter themselves.

We now have a situation in which African-American college graduates can major in business, law, medicine, computer science, engineering, etc. In contrast, it is difficult to be motivated to enter the teaching profession where an entry level position may pay $14,000 - $20,000, while other professions have entry level positions paying $25,000 - $35,000.

Let's look at some of what's being done to correct this problem. For example, we have had a shortage of math and science teachers. In response, standards in these subject areas have been relaxed or altered. People versed in math, science, accounting, engineering and related fields were allowed to teach even though they lacked an education degree. They were also encouraged or required (over time) to obtain a teaching certificate. In other cases they were employed—sometimes through matching grants or paid leaves of absence from their private sector employers—as resource people to provide the kind of expertise and skills needed in math and science classrooms. Black professionals should seriously consider entering the educational field in this manner, because it may not result in a salary reduction so they're in no danger of losing the pay level they earned.

Recruitment and scholarship programs are admirable efforts to increase the number of Black teachers. I like the work being done by the National Education Association to publicize the shortage of teachers and promote the value of teaching, even among children in elementary schools. We need to recruit teachers before youth become high school seniors. A number of different organizations provide scholarships for students interested in pursuing a teaching career. We need to utilize these and other organizations—such as Black churches, fraternities and sororities, colleges, and professional groups—in recruitment and scholarship drives. Their members can work their own grapevines to promote the idea of teaching. It's very disappointing to have so many African-Americans unemployed and so many positions to fill in the classroom.

We also need to focus our attention on the need to increase the number of Black male teachers. We must stress to Black males —perhaps through sessions with the groups just mentioned— that a Black boy can often attend school for nine years without having one Black male teacher. We should sell the idea that it's Black men's responsibility to save an endangered species. Black men should consider teaching, even if it's only for one year. Black male teachers who are currently at the upper grade or high school level should be encouraged to teach an earlier grade, even just for one year, because young children also need a positive male role model in their daily lives.

Other countries such as Japan, Germany, and Great Britain offer lessons for us. In these nations, teachers are respected and many of them are male. We need to study what is done in these countries which we can adapt. We should also look at the public schools in cities like Rochester, New York, where an instructor can become a "master teacher" and earn up to $72,000. That salary level brings with it some major requirements and responsibilities. Rochester holds its teachers accountable for their salaries. Master teachers assume more responsibility, work with "at risk" youth, demonstrate their performance level, train new teachers, work twelve months, and help develop curriculum. This kind of responsibility is similar to private enterprise; when talent, skill, and experience are demonstrated and evaluated, the pay level increases accordingly. I think Black professionals will enter the teaching force in much greater numbers if strategies like these are implemented nationwide.

CURRICULUM

Q: What is a multicultural curriculum?

A: The prefix "multi" means "many." A multicultural curriculum attempts to encompass children of many cultures, races, and ethnic groups. It means, for instance, that Black history will not be confined to February, Hispanic history to May, and Native American history to October.

An excellent author of books about multicultural education is James Banks. He points out that with a multicultural curriculum, the world is no longer seen through one set of eyes, but through African, Asian, European, South American, and Native American eyes. We can then discover what everyone has to say about any given historical or contemporary event. Generally, with multicultural studies the EVENT is the central focus, not WHITE PEOPLE.

Multicultural studies can be visualized as a wheel. The event being studied is at the center, and the many cultures of the world are like the wheel's spokes. As a young person learns about the event, he or she encounters many different perspectives around the "wheel," or the world, to see what all these cultures have to say about the event.

For example, if the event in question concerns Columbus coming to the Americas, through European eyes he discovered America. Native American eyes saw them discover him, because they were already there. Africans would say they, too, had already journeyed to the Americas, as early as 800 B.C.—almost 2300 years before Columbus. We know this from archeological evidence at Mexican pyramids, revealed by authors such as Ivan Van Sertima.

Another example is slavery. Europeans would say that slavery helped build the United States' economy and "civilize" Africans. Africans would say the Black family was almost destroyed by slavery. Slavery should not be merely discussed, but indicted as we do when the Jewish holocaust is introduced. When we mention George Washington or Thomas Jefferson, we should not describe them in glowing terms; we should point out that they were slave owners who looked the other way when it came to true liberty.

Q: What does "culturally disadvantaged" mean?

A: The word "disadvantaged" is a value judgment that shows the insensitivity and arrogance of people who use it. Normally the term refers to cultures outside of America's mainstream. The term is a contradiction, because the synonym for culture is lifestyle and everyone has a lifestyle.

When Robert Williams created a Black intelligence test (called B.I.T.C.H.), he found that White students experienced great difficulty with the test. There are two ways of looking at this. If we're going to have a monolithic attitude and believe that "our" way is the "right" way and the culture of our school is the right culture, every child must master that information and culture and any child who doesn't is culturally disadvantaged. But once we acknowledge and appreciate every group's culture, no one is disadvantaged unless they are denied the right to have their own culture.

Q: What is "Black culture"?

A: Some people believe that we don't have a culture, because it was lost through slavery and acculturation. Many middle income African-Americans associate Black culture with ghetto life. I don't believe that.

There's a story about a multiethnic class I'd like to tell you. The teacher asked the children to return the next day in their native attire and bring a native dish of food. The Hispanic, German, and

Asian children did this, but the African American students didn't know what to do. They wore blue jeans and T-shirts and brought hamburgers and french fries.

There is some ambiguity about what exactly is Black culture. I believe there are some cultural components still within and among us. The word "culture" brings to mind religion, values, family structure, clothing and hairstyles, food, flag, allegiance, language, literature, music, holy days, and entertainment. If we use these as benchmarks, there are several Black cultural expressions and traditions that correlate.

The first area is "ethos," a philosophy or world view. In Black culture our history begins in Africa, not the United States, and it begins long before 1619 when we were first brought here. One of the world's highest civilizations was in Egypt. In terms of religion, we were the first to believe in one God, under the leadership of the Egyptian king Akhenaten. Monotheism originated in Africa. We have long believed in life after death. One doesn't build temples and pyramids if one doesn't believe in life after death. That is part of our culture.

It is also our philosophical nature to be in harmony with people and wildlife. We are a xenophilous people; we are comfortable with strangers. Cheikh Anta Diop points out that some cultures are not comfortable with strangers—people who do not look or act like them—and they are xenophobic. When Europeans and Asians traveled to Africa, we provided them with food and shelter. We were not xenophobic toward them. They, on the other hand, reacted mainly with fear or hatred toward our ancestors.

Much of our culture can be traced to our African roots. Our values, the belief in "we-ness," cooperation, and the inner self, as well as the Nguzo Saba (an African American value system also known as the "Seven Principles of Blackness") are values we have held as a group for centuries. In terms of family structure, we believe in the extended family. Our aunts, uncles, grandparents, and other elders are important to us. We have always liked wearing bright colors and taking pride in what we wear. The gele, dashiki, and loppa are items of clothing commonly worn in Africa which some of us still wear. Many of us still value the natural hairstyle and cornrows (which are not french braids or the "Bo

Derek look").

Our allegiance to our culture was once described for us by one of our heroes, Marcus Garvey: "Here's to this flag of mine, the red, black, and green." We have a Black national anthem, written by James Weldon Johnson, "Lift Every Voice and Sing." We have a unique language, not only based in Africa (such as the Swahili language) but also our creative Black dialect. We have our own traditions in literature, authored by Gwendolyn Brooks, Toni Morrison, James Baldwin, and many others. Our love for music, and our gifts of gospel, soul, and jazz are a part of Black culture which we have freely given the world.

We also have holy days, not holidays, because holidays only give you a good time for the present but holy days teach you why you came together (history) and inspire you for the future. Examples of some of our holy days are: January 15 (King's birthday), the month of February (Black Liberation Month), May 19 (Malcolm X's birthday), the last Saturday in May (African Liberation Day), June 19 (Juneteenth, celebrating the end of slavery), August 17 (Marcus Garvey's birthday), and the last week in December (Kwanzaa).

The term "innerattainment" is part of African culture. We believe that innerattainment connects the performer and the audience and everyone is involved. When the drummer plays the people dance. When the minister preaches the congregation participates in a call and chant approach with no separation between the audience and the presenter. That's all part of Black culture. To reiterate: religion, family, clothing and hairstyles, food, flag, allegiance, anthem, language, literature, music, holy days, and innerattainment are all part of Black culture.

If the Black students in the multiethnic class had known more about their culture, they would have known what to do. They might, for instance, have brought curried chicken, peas, okra, watermelon, or mangoes, just to name a few of our favorite dishes. They might have worn geles, loppas, and dashikis, and perhaps they might also have brought a red, black, and green flag to symbolize the values we share and respect.

Q: What are your views about Black English?

A: I think Black English is a legitimate dialect. It has rules and can be understood. In a court case in Ann Arbor, Michigan, a parent sued the local school district and won. With the help of professor and author Geneva Smitherman the parent convinced the judge that Black English is a legitimate form of language. The judge ruled that Black English not only needed to be acknowledged but it also needs to be understood without an accompanying negative value judgment. Therefore, a teacher should allow a child to converse either in Black English or standard English, without fear of condemnation.

Can you imagine what it must be like being a five-year-old child speaking what's been heard at home — Black English — and being condemned on your first day of school? You've done more than condemn the language, you're now damaging the child's self-esteem. Teachers who understand the dialect would be better prepared to help children use Black English, standard English, or any other form of the language.

Shavi Ali has just written a book we're publishing that reinforces this viewpoint. During her research, she had some children write or speak in their natural dialect and then rewrite the paragraph in standard English. Many African-American adults are bilingual, but our children need help to become bilingual.

Foundations for Learning in Denver has also published books and manuals that take into consideration the richness of Black dialect. The organization urges children to use their own language and motivates them to write. Foundations for Learning is based on the concept of taking children where they are with their culture and using language arts — writing, speaking, reading, and listening — to develop a relevant curriculum.

I find it very interesting that adults who just received college degrees or just spoke Black English in the office hallway moments earlier, condemn Black youth for using this dialect. Those same people who are part of the middle class forget that they're still code switching. They speak Black and standard English. All we have to do is teach our children the same process of code switching without putting a negative connotation on Black English.

I would also suggest reading Eleanor Orr's book, *Twice as Less*. The book discusses the issue of whether Black English hinders comprehension of math and science. The phrase "twice as less" doesn't make mathematical sense, but it brings to mind the cultural connotations of certain mathematical terms. For instance, many African-American children use "twice" and "half" interchangeably. Furthermore, they encounter lots of key words in math problems, such as "from, by, to, between, into, and, half, twice, as," and "than." Although eight from six does not equal eight minus six, there are children who become confused about math because they understand the term "from" to mean the same as "minus." Orr suggests the better we understand Black English, the more effectively we can assist African-American youth in math and science.

Q: How can we reduce illiteracy in the Black community?

A: As you know, we have a very serious illiteracy problem. Forty-two percent of all Black and Hispanic children 17 years of age can't read beyond the sixth grade level and over 27 million Americans are illiterate, reports Jonathan Kozol in his book *Illiterate America.*

There are a number of ways to reduce illiteracy. Rudolph Flesch mentioned in his book, *Why Johnny Can't Read,* that schools have moved more and more to the sight approach to reading, in which children connect pictures with words. Teachers also use more word approach or word repetition, in which a book has a reduced number of words and students repeat them more often to learn them. Those are not the most effective ways to teach reading. The ideal strategy is through phonics; when children have the skills to attack a word they can pronounce over 44,000 words by the end of third grade. We believe in the phonetic approach to teach reading. It's quite ironic that most remedial reading programs rely on phonics. My premise is, if it's the best approach, why not use it before a problem arises?

Of course there are other problems with regard to illiteracy. Some homes do not have books or other reading material. You can't expect children to read when they do not see their parents reading. When you have a household that is more dependent on electronic media (radio, television, and stereo), quite naturally books, newspapers, and magazines are not going to be used as much. Illiteracy will remain a problem because we don't have enough homes that encourage quiet time. It's very difficult to read with noise all around you. Last but not least, I think we also need to look at the content of children's reading material. Why would children want to read books that do not include their culture and environment? We need to offer books that glorify their culture and inform children about their heritage. Some of our children do not know how to read and yet are in the upper grades. They need to read books that are high content and low skill.

Q: How can we make curriculum more relevant for African-American youth?

A: One of the concerns our children have always had is, "How does this relate to my world?" Children would love to ask their teachers why they are required to learn. I don't think that's an unfair question because if they have to sit there and learn the information, teachers should at least be able to explain why it is important. Teachers should show some correlation between a theory articulated in the classroom and its applicability.

One effective idea would be to have students research and develop a family tree, because it lends itself to various subjects such as history, English, and geography. Children would be much more likely to appreciate history when they're encouraged, for example, to investigate their own family's circumstances and location during certain eras. They could also trace, when they create a family tree, the different neighborhoods, cities, and states inhabited by their ancestors. English could be used to let students record — in writing or orally — different anecdotes from elders or a summary of their family's special events. In terms of geography, they could draw maps and indicate ancestral home sites. (The latter is extremely important for right brain relational learners who need to see a visual representation of information to better understand it.) These kinds of curricular approaches demonstrate to children that classroom material is relevant to their own world.

Q: What is the distinction between Negro and African history?

A: There are a number of distinctions between Negro and African history. One of them involves the historian's objective. If you want to make a people docile, you write a history that shows they accepted slavery; that's Negro history. If you want to inspire the reader and show a people's resistance to injustice and pride in their past, then that's African history. Some people would say that Negro history does not exist because there are no Negroes. Others would say you need Negroes in order to have Negro history.

Other distinctions have to do with geography. Negro history is confined to the United States. African history is wherever Africans are in the world. Another distinction concerns how much time teachers allocate toward it. Negro history is primarily taught in February and focuses on names, dates, and events. We call that "contribution history." African history is taught 10-12 months of the year and is concerned with concepts, mistakes, and strengths. By learning African history, students understand which mistakes need to be reduced and which strengths need to be reinforced.

I think the major distinction between Negro and African history is time. Negro history started in 1619 and African history started four million years ago. There's a historical law that states when you start will determine where you end up. If you start in 1619 you start on a plantation and end up in a ghetto. If you start four million years ago you start at the beginning of human life and end up being free.

I've often wondered why many of our youth are embarrassed discussing slavery, but the Jews are not embarrassed discussing the Holocaust. I think the answer lies in where we start teaching our youth. Our children are embarrassed about slavery because that's the point at which they first learned about their history. Many schools teach Negro history like this: The first day's material focuses on our time in Africa, the second day focuses on the boats bringing us to America, and the third day and the rest of the course covers slavery in America. We are the only race that introduces our children to their history by limiting them to a dismal era called slavery. Every other race's history is introduced by describing a moment of glory. Whites introduce history with ancient Greece and that's okay for them. If they want to glorify Hippocrates, Alexander, Aristotle, Pythagoras, and the rest that's fine, but that's not okay for us because Greece is not the origin of our civilization. Our civilization started in Africa and our zenith was in Egypt. Hippocrates was not the first doctor. Hippocrates

was born 700 B. C. and the Egyptian Imhotep, the first doctor, was born 2800 B. C. If you read every state's Hippocratic Oath — which doctors must recite before they are officially made physicians — the oath includes Imhotep's Greek name, Aesculapius. The Greeks made it easy for us, they simply changed the name. Napoleon did more than change a name. His 21-gun salute was his army trying to shoot the nose and lips off Egypt's Great Sphinx and pyramids.

If you really want to teach history properly, connect the past with the present and the future; focus less on lists of names, dates, events, and accomplishments. So, in teaching about Dr. King, you're not concerned with just when he was born (1929), when he went to Washington, D. C. (1963), when he received the Nobel Prize (1964), or when he died (1968). You begin to ask students open-ended questions such as: If King were alive today, what kind of relationship would he have with Jesse Jackson and the Rainbow Coalition? Where would King stand in terms of South Africa — would he support Desmond Tutu or the A.N.C., and why would he have that viewpoint? I think if we present history in this manner, we'll be able to inspire our children. The ultimate objective of history is not only to encourage them to think, but to inspire them to greatness.

Q: What is the relationship between curriculum, standardized tests, and racial biasness?

A: Numerous instances point to the biasness of both I.Q. tests and national achievement tests, not only in terms of discrimination against African-Americans, but women as well. Recent studies have shown that White female high school students had higher GPAs than White male students, but they scored lower on the ACT and SAT and consequently were either denied admittance to certain colleges or scholarships.

The same situation applies as it relates to Propositions 48 and 42. Proposition 48 required a 2.0 GPA and a 15 or 700 on the ACT or SAT respectively. If these were not fulfilled, a scholarship could be awarded, but the student could not play the freshman year. Proposition 42 denies the scholarship. In numerous studies students that have not scored well on standardized tests have been allowed to go to college and have done very well. Students have also done well on the tests yet have not graduated from college. So these two propositions do not guarantee success in college or the ability to get a degree.

The California Black Psychologists Association has been so vocal and specific about the discriminatory elements of I.Q. tests that they recommended the tests be outlawed from use with African-American youth and it was approved. Questions on these tests can be extremely culturally biased. For example, What was Washington's first name? From a White perspective the answer is George, but from the African world view it could be Booker or Harold. A question such as what color is a banana depends upon your neighborhood. You may choose to say it's green, yellow, or brown and still be correct.

America is a test taking country. In order to keep your job as a teacher in many states you have to take a test. Numerous teachers, especially in Arkansas, are losing their positions because they were unable to pass the test. I mentioned previously that if a student cannot master the requirements of a test, he or she may not be able to receive a scholarship. Many school districts have reduced the 180-day school year down to taking and passing a test. Many teachers, under the pressure of only being evaluated in this manner, have chosen to teach the test. Unfortunately in order to succeed in a nation that requires high test scores to progress from magnet school, to college, to graduate school, and then to receive a license in accounting, law, medicine, etc., many African-American children must master test taking or they are not going to do well. There are many children who have great potential and have not done well in the classroom, but they believe all they have to do is produce on test day. I'm not saying we should eliminate tests, but I do think we need to look at an overall approach because one test may not be the best way to properly evaluate our students.

Unfortunately, alternatives to these culturally biased tests, such as the Black Intelligence Test or the kind of research coming out of Foundations for Learning, have not been accepted by the mainstream. One major reason is that testing is a large and firmly entrenched industry. At this point we have to prepare teachers and students to become versed at test taking.

I do want to return to the first part of your question as it relates to curriculum, because there is a relationship between curriculum and these tests. Let's use as an example, two students attending two different high schools. One student takes algebra the first year, geometry the second year, trigonometry the third year, and pre-calculus the fourth year. The other student goes to another school and takes basic math and algebra one. Obviously the second student will not be as well versed or do as well on achievement tests or college entrance exams as the first student. So differences in curriculum requirements at the two schools will greatly affect students' test scores.

Secondly, there has been research pointing out that two courses the African-American student does not do well in are calculus and statistics. Those students who have been able to take calculus in high school, or college students who understood that calculus and statistics might be difficult for them, created support services and tutorial opportunities or took calculus during the summer. These students tried to get in classes with teachers they could understand, since, unfortunately, many are taught by Asians. Calculus and statistics are two courses for African-American students to overcome, and we've got to look at that because we're losing students in terms of college graduation because of calculus.

We need to look at the two schools of thought on how to prepare a child for a test. In many low income families, parents tell their children the night before the test to get a good night's sleep, eat a big breakfast in the morning—that will put them back to sleep,—and then they offer a word of encouragement. In contrast, other families go beyond recommending sleep, breakfast, and encouragement. They give their children a copy of the test. Random House sells a version of the Iowa test for $3.95. Besides schools teaching the test, parents can also teach the test.

Many of our children do not have good test taking skills. For example, they may have trouble finishing an exam. They have not been taught that if they do not know the answer to a particular question, they should mark it, and continue; then if time allows, they should return to the unanswered question. Many of our children "choke" under the pressure of being timed while taking a test. Homes and schools that regularly expose children to time-related tests do much better. Good test takers have been taught to look for code words such as "never," "always," "none," "some," and "all of the above." On many achievement tests the first answer is designed to look like the correct answer and unversed students don't bother to look at the subsequent choices. In reality, the last answer might have included parts of the first and one or two of the other possible answers. But if a student selects the first answer he or she might not read the remaining choices. Good test takers read the last answer first. Then again, some children do not work well with answer sheets. If it's their first time, many put the answer in the wrong box; then all the following answers will be wrong also. Our children need practice with answer sheets and testing as a whole.

Research also has shown that students who take the ACT or SAT more than once score higher. Many African-Americans don't even take the test, and when they do, they take it in the latter portion of their senior year. Ideally, students should take the PSAT in their freshman or sophomore year, the SAT and ACT in the junior year, and once again at the beginning of senior year. We must have more counselors and parents moving our children into that mode.

Q: With the increase of African-Americans in authoritative positions within our school districts, why is curriculum still difficult to change?

A: This question shows your astuteness. We now have African American superintendents, principals, and teachers in most of our major school districts; yet the curriculum has remained unchanged. Columbus still discovered America, Lincoln was still the slaves' best friend, and Hippocrates remains the first doctor. This is a real tragedy throughout the country. However, I'm optimistic about the kind of progress made in Portland with that school system's "Base Line" essays and in Washington, D. C. with "Operation Know Thyself." I am also hopeful because of the kind of efforts made in Chicago and Atlanta to inculcate into the curriculum an Afrocentric perspective. These are "drops in the bucket" and even in these cities, where some alternative curriculum materials are approved, teachers in many cases can choose whether to use them. This in my opinion shows a lack of leadership.

I've been told by superintendents that they are aware of the fallacies in the curriculum; they acknowledge it's Eurocentric, but due to limited financial resources they have been unable to replace those books. At one level that answer is ludicrous. For me to accept the reason why Columbus discovered America is because of limited resources negates the fact that handouts can be photocopied, teachers can orally point out the errors in a textbook, and the reality is that large White-controlled publishing companies have an enormous amount of clout. In many of our school districts we can have a dropout rate of 40-50%, as is the case in most inner-city areas, but Random House, Doubleday, Ginn, Scott Foresman and other corporations continue to receive large contracts.

Superintendents have also told me that with the myriad of problems they have to address – lack of funding, organization, teacher accountability, school strikes, and teacher unions' power – curriculum has not been a major issue on their agenda. I think we're going to have to look again at that or appoint someone from the superintendent's office to look at that; we're losing too many children because the curriculum is irrelevant to their needs and culture.

LEARNING STYLES

Q: How are most children taught in school?

A: John Goodlad, in an exhaustive study, *A Place Called School,* noted two observations of classrooms: children were either passively listening to teachers lecture, or they were answering questions from dittos. That's unfortunately how most children are taught in the classroom.

Q: What exactly is the "split brain" theory and can you describe how that translates to different methodologies of learning within the classroom?

A: The brain is divided into two hemispheres, the left and the right. The left hemisphere is analytical, separates items and breaks things down into parts. It is geared more toward logic and is very helpful in subjects such as math and science. The right side of the brain is relational, sees the larger picture and is also intuitive and emotional. It is geared more toward music and sports.

There are at least five ways to present an idea in the classroom: through writing, oral stories, pictures, fine arts, and artifacts or objects. Writing is left brain-oriented, and all the rest are geared more toward the right hemisphere. From the fourth grade on, most instructors use a left brain methodology with large numbers of right brain thinking children.

Q: Can you give examples of right and left brain lesson plans?

A: An example of a left brain lesson plan would be to read a definition and write the definition. Another example of a left brain lesson plan would be teaching someone how to dance by using floor mats and numbering them, and then having the child move from one mat to another.

Examples of right brain lesson plans would include an arithmetic exercise using an abacus (so a child actually uses an object to count), drawing, an experiment using observation, creating a song or describing a series of personal experiences.

The objective, though, is not to go from one extreme to the other but instead to offer whole brain lessons that draw from both hemispheres. An example of a whole brain lesson plan would be for children to read a definition and draw what they think they've read. Another example would be the coordination of music and raps with phonics and math. We distribute a product called "Wordbuster Reading Rap" which blends the strength of music and rap with rules of phonics. I believe that if our children can memorize all those words from a rap record, which I recognize is a skill, they can remember whatever we present in that same format.

Q: Do children learn in different ways? If so, are there differences in learning styles among the races and sexes?

A: The answer to the first question is yes. Children do learn in different ways. Whether we are willing to teach a child in other ways is another issue.

The second question is a lot more complex. Some people who are now on the learning style "bandwagon" want to simply assert that all African-American children are right brain thinkers, all European-American children are left brain thinkers, all males are left brain thinkers, and all females are right brain thinkers. Combining race and gender makes simplistic analysis more complex. We cannot say all African-American teachers are good for Black children and all European-American teachers are bad. Nor can we say that all Black children are right brain thinkers and all White children are left brain learners. There is so much variation within the races and sexes that I cannot give blanket answers.

A major objective is to acknowledge that we have more right brain thinkers than we are willing to admit. A large portion of them are African-American children and we need to be perceptive of their learning styles. Janice Hale Benson, Asa Hilliard, Amos Wilson and several other authors and scholars have studied the relationship between learning styles and race. Culture, institutional racism, and sexism seem to be leading contributors to children learning in different ways. Nevertheless, children's innate ability in art, music, sports, science, math, memory, etc., transcends race and gender. A recent televised documentary on the Black athlete was another failure attempting to separate nature from nurture. If Black children are encouraged and allowed to participate in sports but are stifled in math and science, how can anyone state that African-Americans are superior in sports and deficient in academics?

Environmental factors also affect learning styles. For instance, if a child grows up in a culture where music and art are valued and all around him or her drummers and radios are playing, there's a very good chance that the child will be well versed in music. On the other hand, if a child's primary experiences of memorization come from records rather than books, that child will process information more effectively through the medium of recordings. A child who grows up in a household with several siblings, very little quiet time, and a multiplicity of activities has a greater affinity toward learning where there is noise, a number of activities occurring, and other children present. Then again, if a child grows up in a society that encourages him or her to play basketball or sing and dance, and the child does not see computer programmers or engineers in the immediate neighborhood — nor science, computer, and language arts centers — but is inundated with basketball courts, there's a very good chance the child will be more versed in sports and music than math, science, and language arts.

The combination of institutional racism and culture have produced large numbers of African American children with strength on the right side of the brain. In contrast, a child who grows up in a household where there are more books than records, where there is one child in the home, where only one activity happens at a time, where engineers and computer programmers live nearby, and where there are science labs, tutorial programs, and computers in the home and community, will be well versed with a left brain methodology.

Suppose one family takes their child to the toy store and they buy their child a plane that is already assembled. The child takes the plane out of the box with little appreciation for the parts that were used to put the plane together. He or she throws the plane around the room and at some point it will not fly. Another family takes their child to the same toy store and they buy their child a plane with 100 different parts to assemble. The child diligently puts all the parts together. He or she also appreciates that any part not in order will affect the ability of this plane to fly. When this child finally puts the pieces together, he or she will be very careful about throwing it across the room because the child is aware that any defective part will affect the whole.

That scenario best describes what can easily go on within a Black or White household. One has a more holistic approach and the other a more analytical approach. The relationship between culture and learning styles is a significant factor to consider in the overall achievement of children.

Q: Why are most schools, and specifically teachers, not creating a better mix between their methodology and children's learning styles?

A: I think the first step in solving any problem is to be aware it exists. Many teachers are for the very first time being exposed to the "split brain" theory and its relationship to learning styles, so they're just beginning to understand its implications for their classroom lesson plans. Consequently, many teachers are ill prepared to teach right brain lesson plans because they were not given that kind of information when they were undergraduates.

We have a situation in which approximately 50% of the children in the American school system are still doing pretty well, all things considered. For some people, especially those in decision making positions, the view may be that only 50% are not doing well versus the school district taking a critical look at itself and acknowledging the unacceptability of this proportion. A lot of people operate on the perspective that if they can just "save one" they're satisfied. In my opinion, they expect very little, especially when you consider the average classroom has thirty children. Some think this is acceptable. In my view, if I just "lose one" I'm in trouble, which shows higher expectations. Looking at this issue in more detail, the question becomes CAN teachers teach children who have strengths on the right side of the brain, or are teachers WILLING to teach children who have strengths on the right side of the brain?

For many teachers, it's ability (can), know-how, and information; and for others it's attitude (willingness). Many schools mandate conformity. Suppose a class has four groups of students, middle and low income, African- and European-Americans. The teacher reads the children a story. At the conclusion of the story the teacher wants the children to share their reactions. The European-American students—both middle and lower income—and the middle income African-American students repeat the story to the teacher exactly the way he or she read it to them. Rote learning and memorization are taking place. The lower income African-American students add more characters, make it more dramatic, add their own phrases, and use body language to act it out. If we only valued memorization, three groups would receive a good grade; but if we also valued other ways of learning besides rote then the last group would also receive a good grade. In most American schools the last group would not receive a passing grade.

Children come to the classroom with their own individuality. We need to first of all acknowledge, understand, and develop compatible, appropriate lesson plans.

Q: What is the role of universities in preparing teachers as it relates to learning styles? What are your overall feelings about their preparation of teachers going into the inner city?

A: I'm very disappointed in the role universities are playing because they have so much potential and many resources to offer. Unfortunately, I speak to teachers who are already in the classroom. But the best time for me to in-service teachers is at the undergraduate level.

Many professors have not kept up with the times or because of institutional racism are not very concerned with the African-American child. Very few education departments have a course on the African-American child, because there is still a tendency to treat children as children and not acknowledge their cultural and racial differences and how that affects the classroom. At the very least, because of the shortage of African-American teachers, higher education should address that with more scholarships and greater recruitment efforts.

Many universities prepare teachers-to-be for an ideal classroom of 28 students—four rows across, seven students in each row, and all 28 students are eager and willing to learn and are on the same grade level in every subject. They do not prepare future teachers for 30 plus students in a classroom where seating and materials may be tight, the children's abilities may span from three to five different levels on any given subject, and they are more interested in the streets than school. In addition, children's learning style is often relational and holistic. The university simply has not prepared teachers for that situation. It is not only a tragedy for the overall system and each child, but I think it also contributes to "teacher burnout" because teachers who go into inner city areas are not properly equipped and are leaving the profession long before retirement age. If we'd prepare them better we'd have more stability in the field.

SPECIAL EDUCATION

Q: Do you acknowledge that children have different energy levels?

A: Yes, international and national studies have shown that African and African-American infants tend to be more advanced physiologically than others. The ability to hold the head erect, walk, recognize movement and colors have all been documented by doctors all over the world; generally speaking, African-American children develop faster than other children. It seems very interesting as we look at the American educational system that African-American children are being diagnosed as genetically inferior. The best time to measure natural talent is within the first five years; after that you're really testing what children have been exposed to. You're no longer measuring innate intelligence or ability but exposure to what's been given to them at school and home. I do acknowledge that children have different energy levels and research supports the tendency of African-American children to have higher energy levels than other children.

Q: What is a hyperactive child?

A: The word "hyperactive" is a value judgment which has to be compared to a norm to be accurate. Many teachers do not acknowledge that children have different energy levels. For example, researchers at Ohio State University conducted a study on children who watched two television programs, "Mr. Rogers' Neighborhood" and "Sesame Street." They found White children responded better to "Mr. Rogers" and African-American children

responded better to "Sesame Street." From the fourth grade on the classroom takes the pace of "Mr. Rogers." It may not be that Black children are necessarily hyperactive by nature, but that the classroom methodology is paced too slowly. On the other hand, home and school might effect a compromise: Parents could institute more quiet time for their children's home schedule, and teachers could involve children more actively in classroom instruction. In the interim, children with high energy levels may be misdiagnosed as hyperactive.

Q: Why are there disproportionate numbers of Black youth in special education?

A: Black children nationwide are 17% of all children in public schools but are 41% of all children in special education. Of the African American children in special education, 85% of them are Black males. The federal law, passed in 1964, established special education classes and was never designed to be exploited in this way. The law—designed primarily for children with hearing or vision problems or who lacked a limb—was to ensure equal protection so these children could receive a quality education. However, special education has become a dumping ground for children who are "hyperactive," have behavior problems or unmet emotional needs, or may not be liked by school authorities. There are children who can be with a good third grade teacher and do very well but in fourth grade may be considered for special education. I think the major reason why there is a disproportionate number of Black youth in special education is because there is a lack of appreciation for different learning styles, and if Black children cannot fit the norm they are placed in special education.

Q: Why is there such disparity between White girls and Black boys being placed in special education, with White girls having the least chance for special education and Black boys having the greatest chance?

A: We're very concerned about this phenomenon. As I mentioned earlier, if a Black child is placed in special education, 85% of the time it is a Black boy; we're concerned about why it's not 50/50, Black boys and girls. We're even more concerned with the fact that children with the least chance to be assigned to special education are White girls and those with the greatest chance are African American males.

Is the system implying that White females make the most ideal students and the least favored students are African American males? Do African American males have to act like White girls to remain in a mainstream classroom? What exactly can we learn from Britain and Germany, which have more male teachers and more girls in special education classes than boys? Do Germany and Britain have fewer boys in special education because they have more male teachers? Does the teacher have to look like the child to better educate the child? What is it about the classroom interaction between White female teachers and Black boys that makes them have the least understanding?

We are at a serious stage with this situation. A major reason why Black boys are placed in special education is because so many teachers don't appreciate the idea that children learn in different ways and they bond less with children who don't look like them. There are also many teachers who are AFRAID of Black boys. Remember, previously I said you have to love, respect, and understand their culture. You CANNOT teach a child you fear. Another major reason for the disparity is because Black boys have very few positive Black male role models. Approximately 1.5% of public school teachers are Black men.

Q: What has been the success of special education for African-American youth?

A: An article in the October, 1987 issue of *Harvard Educational Review* documents the ways special education may not be so special. What may be significant about special education is African-American children attend more and longer than anybody else, and they do not return to regular classrooms on grade level. More specifically, the success of special education for Black youth has been minimal. There have been Black youth who have benefited but this has not been commensurate with their numbers. We encourage parents to be very careful during determination meetings. The most important meeting of your child's life is the one that will decide whether your child will be placed in special education. We encourage parents, if they lack the information or confidence to be assertive at this meeting, to hire a Black psychologist, social worker, or educator to represent them.

Normally those meetings are attended by the principal, classroom teacher, school psychologist, and social worker all telling the parent to sign on the dotted line to have the child placed in special education. We have to be very alert in meetings like that because they may likely determine our children's entire future. I've heard horror stories where school employees have actually been in cahoots with each other; regardless of whether an individual social worker, psychologist, or teacher favored the placement, everyone cooperated for the sake of a unified position rather than focusing on the child's needs.

Q: How can we reduce the number of African-American youth in special education and the length of time they spend there?

A: First we need mandatory in-service training for teachers in Black and Black male culture and the implications for their learning styles. Just because Black boys do not fit what is perceived as the "ideal" student should not create this disproportionality. Secondly, I think we need to look at the fact that 5% of the teachers make 30% of the referrals; the problem may not be with the boys, but with these teachers. What may be a better solution is either the in-service or removal of these teachers. Unfortunately, because teachers have a union and the boys don't, the boys are placed in special education rather than the teachers receiving in-service training. Third, if we examine the Detroit school system, which has been using the Feurstein Model, we'll find what occurs when the burden of proof is put on the school and not the child. With this model, a child viewed as being at risk of special education placement is not initially assigned there; instead, the child receives individualized attention and remains in the regular classroom. The objective is to keep the child in the regular classroom rather than the "trigger-happy" approach of taking the child out and stigmatizing him or her. Lastly, if those three methods cannot be used — mandatory in-service training, looking at the 5% of teachers making the referrals, and utilizing the Feurstein Model — we may need to place a moratorium on special education unless there are extreme physical problems.

DISCIPLINE

Q: Why are some teachers spending more time disciplining children than teaching them?

A: A teacher survey by the National Education Association (NEA) cites discipline as the number one classroom problem in the country. Teachers described three main reasons for disciplinary problems: children have difficulty sitting still, they dislike being touched, and they lack respect for authority.

First of all, I don't think you can discipline a child whom you do not love. Remember, large numbers of African American students are not loved, respected, or understood by their teachers. We talk often about respect and the lack of respect children have for adults. I think the lack of respect is mutual and teachers should not expect children to respect them if they don't respect children. I think children know which teachers love and respect them. When you form a bond with children, many disciplinary problems can be alleviated.

Unfortunately, when we hear the word "discipline," we think of controlling children. But discipline is not an end, it's a means. Children and adults need discipline in order to achieve goals. We have not established goals for children. When children see the need to achieve a goal they will discipline themselves. Many people misuse discipline to control children and not as an instrument by which children can secure their goals.

I think teachers who love children can be more effective in the area of discipline. Teachers with an interesting, relevant curriculum, who allow children to learn in different ways can avoid some disciplinary problems.

Q: More and more schools have security guards, police, metal detectors, and principals with baseball bats. Are these schools or armed camps? What is your opinion of this trend?

A: One of the correlates in the Effective Schools Project is school climate. Schools need to be safe. But it's obvious that many of our schools are not safe, and there has been a need to bring in security guards, police, metal detectors, and armed principals. I don't necessarily believe the principal has to be the warden of a school. Instead, the principal should be the instructional leader and focus on curriculum and testing.

When situations reach a crisis level—such as those that exist in Washington, D. C. with regard to drugs and gangs—America responds by putting more money in prison construction and staffing, versus funding programs that teach culture, self-esteem, and long-term success. Yet research has consistently shown that punitive responses like prison do not work. So when schools institute similarly punitive measures, like security guards and metal detectors, they are putting money—badly needed for instructional programs and teachers' salaries—into band-aid methods that do not address the real problems. We need productive responses such as those developed in the St. Louis and Washington, D. C. public housing projects. In those cities, ownership was transferred to the tenants and a sense of possession and responsibility emerged. When children and adults take ownership of an essential area of their lives, they don't do things like paint graffiti on walls, which indicates a lack of respect. Early on, we have to instill class and school pride into our children so they will respect themselves and their school. There is a program in Chicago that deals with mediation or conflict management. There are many schools in crime ridden neighborhoods. We have youth who are being killed because they stepped on someone's shoe or brushed up against someone in a crowded hallway between classes. Mediation is a program designed for youth. Adult male role models from groups like One Hundred Black Men show youth the distinction between a battle and a war. When you don't like someone stepping on your shoe that's not justification for killing someone. There's a way to show disdain while maintaining dignity and pride.

I think while we may have to use security guards and metal detectors, they should be used only as short-term measures. A long-term program that should be considered is conflict management. Many schools do not have assemblies because ineffective principals say children do not know how to act. Yes, it's true that children will not know how to act during assembly programs if principals do not provide assemblies. I think if we can consistently give children programs that instill pride, use slogans and chants, and show children how to resolve conflicts in a positive way — through nonviolence — there would be a positive change in our youth.

I would love to work with a school district wherein we could use Dr. King's nonviolent approach to resolving conflict. Dr. King does not have to be buried between 1929 and 1968. We need Dr. King's strategy right now so that our youth won't continue to kill each other. This can easily be taught in social studies class and it would make the curriculum more relevant. For schools to have weekly or monthly incidents in which students mourn another victim in their school who was killed and not see that they can use alternative approaches, which have long-term benefits, is unfortunate and a serious mistake.

Q: What is the difference between discipline and punishment?

A: I call discipline stage one and punishment stage two. Many times people use the words discipline and punishment synonymously. Punishment is when a child has already broken the rules and now we're going to pull out the belt, or use other punishments like isolation, denial, security guards, police, and principals walking around with baseball bats.

The real issue is not what you do when the child breaks the rules. It is how you develop self-discipline in a child. The problem may not be with the disciples (children), but with the leaders (adults). The question the leaders should ask is why can't our children accept our rules? If they accept our rules in stage one then we would not need a bat or belt in stage two.

There are a number of reasons why children do not accept our rules. They include peer pressure, strong will, and lack of communication and support. I also think children don't accept our rules because adults are inconsistent role models. Children have a more difficult time when Mother has one rule and Daddy has another, or Mother has one on Monday and a different one on Wednesday. It becomes further complicated when parents say, "Don't do as I do, do as I say." I believe the fundamental problem lies in that all children want attention. Unfortunately, in America you receive more attention by being negative.

Q: Can you describe the various models used in the classroom to discipline students?

A: There are four basic models. They are: behavior modification, assertiveness, communication, and the good old-fashioned belt. Behavior modification reinforces positive behavior. I mentioned previously that children love attention. In a typical classroom of 30 students, in which 28 are behaving well and two are acting up, who receives the attention? The two children acting incorrectly. The 28 children are ignored. With behavior modification being practiced, the 28 students' behavior is reinforced.

I have seen classrooms where teachers write the names on the board of those children who were undisciplined. As early as 9:05, children's names are on the board. I asked teachers if the misbehaving children had any options that would remove their names from the board. Many said, NO. Many children have decided that if they are going to get their names on the board as early as 9:05, they might as well earn the distinction. Very few teachers have a "positive board" where children who are acting very well can be recognized.

The second model is the assertive one, outlined by Lee Canter. In any school or home there are three kinds of adults: unassertive, hostile, and assertive. The unassertive teacher will observe negative behavior and either ignore it or in a very passive way say, "Can you please get back to work." The tone of voice is not very strong and the children do not take the teacher seriously. The hostile teacher observing negative behavior will either say something damaging to the child's self-esteem—and use terms like "idiot, stupid," or "imbecile"—or physically try to move the child. The assertive teacher will use strong eye contact, a commanding tone, and say, "I expect you to get back to work. If you do not there will be serious consequences." This kind of statement and behavior makes it very clear to the child that the teacher means business and the expectation is that the student will get back to work or there will be consequences. The child and the teacher are clear about who's in control. This is the assertive model, and it is effective at home as well. Children have told me they were asked eight times by their mother to empty the garbage before they understood she meant business. On the eighth warning the mother was very assertive. The first seven times she was unassertive, but as soon as she became assertive the child immediately responded. Children know by the tone of your voice when it is time to respond.

The third model I would like to discuss is the communication model. One example of this model is titled "Unity, Criticism, Unity," or "UCU." This model can be implemented in the classroom or home. During a UCU session the objective is to combine communication and peer pressure. The session begins on a positive note that is meant to reflect the unity among the group's members. Children are invited to praise each other. I think this is extremely important. We need to teach children how to praise one another rather than gossip about each other. We must teach children how to praise. Specifically, the UCU session can begin at home with a prayer, song, or chant. Mainly, this type of interaction is designed to introduce a positive spirit to the session. The second phase is criticism, and the way to do it is to criticize the BEHAVIOR, but never the PERSON. Criticism should also be constructive; it should do more than condemn behavior, it should offer a suggestion as to what should have been done. Lastly, the children decide the punishment of a misbehaver. My experience has been that children are harder on each other than adults, and they respect punishment more when it comes from their peers.

The real beauty of the UCU session is the very fact that it exists and becomes a deterrent to unacceptable behavior. Children know, whether they're part of a UCU group at school or home, that they're being judged by their peers. The session also holds adults accountable because the sessions allow children to criticize adults who will not be in a position to say, "Don't do as I do, do as I say." Children really like to point out the contradictions they observe in adults and consequently both age groups work hard to be more responsible.

Previously I made reference to conflict management and mediation as other communication methods that provide children with strategies to resolve conflicts. All this must be taught and the best way to do that is through honest upfront communication.

Lastly, the fourth model is good old-fashioned physical punishment. I believe this method can be effective, but I want to stress that this method belongs in stage two, after the child has already broken the rules. The physical model has been banned in many states because there were many adults who lost control, hit children with dangerous objects, or hit fragile parts of a child's body. Many psychologists are now willing to reconsider their position on corporal punishment. When you take your child to Red Lobster and the child begins to throw plates across the room, that is not the time to ask the child why he did that. There is a time to TOUCH and there is a time to TALK. Many parents have talked their children to death and I think there needs to be a balance between talking and touching, with an understanding that touching should be minimized, especially as the child becomes older. It is imperative to try to get a child to accept the rules in stage one, because the objective is self-discipline not punishment.

BLACK BOYS

Q: Why is there a shortage of adult Black males and where are the available ones?

A: At birth the ratio is 1.03 Black boys to 1.0 Black girls. Eighteen years later there are 1.8 available Black women to 1.0 available Black men, almost a 2 to 1 ratio. If a female wants a Black male who is responsible, well educated, employed, and committed to God and his race the ratio is more like 5 to 1. On many college campuses the ratio of Black female to male students is 4–8 females for every male at the junior and senior levels. Black men are found in much greater numbers in cemeteries, prisons, drug rehabilitation and mental institutions, involved in homosexuality, interracial marriages, and on the streets. It is estimated that by the year 2000, 70% of all Black males will be unavailable.

The reason why this problem exists is complex and interwoven between White male supremacy, overt racism, and institutional racism reinforced by Black apathy and ignorance. We live in a world controlled by men, specifically European men, and they're not afraid of women — Black or White — because women are no threat to men in a patriarchal society. The threat to European men would come from other men, especially men with the most color. Why did European men lynch and castrate African men? A White male in this country with a high school diploma will make more money than anyone else with a college degree, except another white male with a college education.

Q: Why are there more Black men in prison than in college?

A: Forty-seven percent of the prison population is Black males, while only 3.5% of Black males are college students. More and more people are advocating building more prisons without fully understanding that 85% of released inmates return to incarceration. On the other hand, many people are unaware that it costs $2,300 to send a child to Headstart, $7,500 to $10,000 for a college education, and $18,000 to $38,000 for a prison term. Yet the United States government cuts Headstart funds, Chapter I monies and Pell grants for college, and allocates more money to prisons. This country seems to value oppression more than education. When I was young and naive, I used to believe the government did not understand this imbalance, but I've been able to talk with some important policy makers and they do realize they're spending more money on prison than education. They do know education works and prison doesn't, and they still would rather incarcerate than educate — even if it requires more money. It doesn't make good economic sense, but it does oppress people.

Our research has shown the critical time to intervene on behalf of our boys is at the beginning of the fourth grade. We're not saying infancy to age nine is a panacea because African-American males also have the highest infant mortality rate. Previously we mentioned Ray Rist's longitudinal study on tracking and how kindergarten teachers made long lasting decisions about children's academic ability. We looked at the beginning of third grade and noticed the large number of African-American males in the upper percentile in grades K-3 but then noticed a marked decline beginning at the fourth grade. We divided the stages of academic development into: infancy to age nine, ages 9-13, and ages 13-18. It's easy to see a Black male's negative behavior in the third stage; at that point, he's laid up on a corner and lacking direction. It's more difficult to notice it at nine years of age, when Black males begin to sit in the back of the class, ask fewer questions, and cheat on tests.

Many factors come together to contribute to the fourth-grade syndrome. As children become older, parental involvement declines. As the age increases, peer pressure increases. Youth become larger and some teachers become afraid of them because they were using physical size to determine their ability to discipline youth. Also, as youth get older, there is less nurturance, teachers allow less movement in the classroom, and the classroom methodology is geared toward female students. The most important factor, though, is that Black boys can attend grades K-8 and with the exception of physical education, they do not have a single Black male teacher.

Q: How can we reduce the number of Black males placed in special education, lower tracks, and school suspension?

A: In a previous section I discussed the issue of special education. I said we need to have mandatory in-service training for teachers on Black culture, but specifically Black male culture and its implication for learning styles. The in-service training needs to be adequate in length to develop lesson plans using Black culture and Black male culture.

The Feurstein model, used in Detroit, places the burden on the school and the objective is to keep the child in the mainstream classroom. Support services are brought into the classroom rather than placing the child in a special education class. This seems to be an effective model to replicate.

Other methods can be used to reduce the number of Black males in special education. We need to increase the number of Black male staff, other male teachers, and teachers as a whole who respect, love, and understand African-American males. I recommend a moratorium on special education placements for Black youth unless there are auditory, visual, or other physical problems.

To reduce the number of Black boys placed in the lowest academic track we need to abolish tracking entirely. As Rist and Goodlad have pointed out in their research, the gap between the highest and lowest tracks widens over time. Schools should seek additional funding or appeal to the community for additional tutors to address students' academic needs. Community organizations and churches should offer remedial services during after school hours. In addition, cooperative learning groups rather than homogeneous ability grouping would be more beneficial to all students. Concerning school suspensions, I favor in-house suspensions with progressive Black men teaching conflict management, mediation, and discussing Malcolm X, a Black man whose life story is extremely relevant to most Black male youth.

Q: You have developed a Black male classroom in several cities nationwide. Can you describe some of the components of that classroom?

A: It was not our initial desire to create a Black-male classroom. We would have preferred that Black boys remain in a heterosexual class. But because of the phenomenally disproportionate number of Black boys in the lowest academic track and in special education, we felt as long as they're being isolated our desire was to position them as winners rather than losers. We're envisioning a classroom that begins at grade four and we would add a grade each year. Ideally, if funding permits we would start a new group of male fourth graders each year. A Black man would be the homeroom teacher and women would be brought in to teach various subjects. The teacher would be screened to ensure that he is Afro-centric, has demonstrated mastery of subject area to teach, holds high expections of the students, and understands children learn in different ways.

In this class, curriculum would be substantially different than most other classes. African-American history would be taught 10 months of the year instead of just the month of February, and culture is valued, taught, and reinforced. This Black-male classroom would have a whole brain methodology versus an exclusively left or right brain approach. Teachers would be required to present lessons orally, with pictures, fine arts, and objects. We have a lot of "Detroit Reds" in our community. Black boys really respond enthusiastically to reading about Malcolm, Garvey, and King. They simply need adults who realize their potential to become productive men.

This special Black-male class would divide children into cooperative learning groups. We have found that children work better in groups and we'd like to combine cooperation with competition. We want to use their strength and competitive spirit within an academic setting. Cooperative learning is an excellent approach. This classroom would compete in academic contests such as science fairs, spelling bees, debates, etc.

Because of our children's high energy level, we would not make the mistake many schools make of eliminating or reducing physical education. In many schools gym classes only operate once a week. We would offer gym every day and include martial arts, which instills discipline and fitness simultaneously.

In this classroom everyone would play a musical instrument which integrates math and music. There would also be a monthly field trip. The trips would include more than a typical visit to a museum, art institute, and zoo. They would also encompass trips to public hospitals—especially the emergency room on a Saturday night around midnight—and drug abuse programs, so our children can see how painful and difficult it is to withdraw. Our children would also visit prisons and talk with inmates to get first-hand testimonies of incarcerated life, similar to what occurred during the film "Scared Straight." They would also visit businesses and talk to Black business owners about how they got started.

Each classroom would have monthly parent workshops. Many parents are more concerned about what's going on in their child's classroom than they are with the school's budget, personnel changes, and last month's minutes. In terms of another important element of academics, the Black-male classroom would be more conscientious about the meals served to its children. The food would be nutritious and we would remove white products— white sugar, flour, bread, rice, and salt—from the menu. We would reduce or eliminate red meat from the classroom diet and eat primarily vegetarian, seafood, and poultry.

We would also draw upon the strength of some of the curriculum materials from Foundations for Learning, which integrates the child's culture into a language arts curriculum. The phonetic approach would be used to teach reading, and word problems would be used in our math component. All of our subjects would relate to the experiences of our students.

The classroom would also have a science laboratory. Most elementary schools teach science out of a book and that can be very boring, especially to a right brain relational thinker. We'd like to have a science lab where there's more of a hands on approach. Our objective would be a hands on science experience versus reading about planets. We would teach students how their body works, the relationship between food and health, and more contemporary issues like AIDS and what drugs do to the brain. We would also show the relationship between the lab and product development.

We would include a program called SETCLAE (Self-Esteem Through Culture Leads to Academic Excellence), which we'll elaborate on when we discuss questions related to self-esteem. This classroom would also include a junior business league; corporations will adopt the classroom and offer scholarships, after school and summer employment. Hopefully, seeds will be planted among the students that help them develop their own businesses. This classroom will teach test taking skills. America is becoming more and more of a test taking country and we've got to prepare our boys to understand how to take tests.

Q: How can we expose Black boys to more Black male role models?

A: More and more cities have begun to respond to the plight of Black boys and the need for positive role models. When you ask Black boys to name five male athletes or entertainers they have very little difficulty, but when you ask them to name five Black men with college degrees they have problems.

In cities such as Washington, Chicago, St. Louis, Houston, and Columbia (South Carolina), groups have been formed called "One Hundred Black Men." These groups have responded to the needs of Black boys and have gone to schools to interact with boys. After numerous programs where I have spoken, the "One Hundred" paired themselves off with 5-10 Black boys and conducted an intensive follow-up session. The schools involved illustrate their commitment to the process of interaction because they had all the males together, gave me unlimited time, and created a thorough follow-up mechanism. In contrast, many schools give me all the students — male, female, Black and White — forty minutes to speak, and have no follow-up mechanism.

The adult Black males involved in such a program should be both blue and white collar workers. We want to end the debate between Booker T. Washington and W. E. B. DuBois about a supposedly necessary choice to be made between pulling oneself up by one's bootstraps or being part of the "Talented Tenth." We respect both types of skills. We also want Black men to have a positive attitude about being among our male youth and not coming in with a paternalistic attitude of helping "these poor children." The criteria, then, should not be educated men but men of strong character. You can't be a positive role model if you use drugs or are involved with two, three, or more women. Being a role model is more than just degrees, positions, cars, and clothes.

Q: What are the rites of passage into manhood?

A: In Africa, we were very clear when Black boys became men through various levels of achievement. But now boys don't know when they become men. Rites of passage into adulthood is a process rooted in the community. The community sanctions a boy's mastery of various requirements and it bestows the honor of manhood on a boy.

There are about 50 rites of passage programs nationwide. These programs work with Black boys on an ongoing, regular basis and teach them the criteria for manhood. Upon satisfactory completion of a program, the boys participate in a moving ceremony in front of their peers, family, and the larger community. The rites of passage program established minimal standards of what we felt boys needed for manhood in order to receive this honor. These criteria include: understanding of African history, spirituality, economics, politics, career development, citizenship, community involvement, physical development, operating with an African frame of reference, and belief in the Nguzo Saba, a Black value system.

Rites of passage programs attempt to teach boys with varied methodologies. For example, during the economics component the boys may learn how to read the stock market pages, and explain the distinction between a passbook account, certificate of deposit, and a money market account. They also may be required to operate and understand the family budget and how to develop a business plan. In history, they may have to acquire some understanding of ancient Egypt, the origin of civilization, and demonstrate the correlation between Imhotep and Dr. Charles Drew. They may be asked to volunteer ten hours of work to a community organization. Each individual program develops its own lesson plans for each element of the program. The culminating ceremony utilizes the youth's input and should also include African dress, cultural entertainment, food, and elders. I would suggest inviting the media to the final ceremony. The media report our murders without notice, but seldom do they respond to a press release issued a month in advance of a culmination of our youth's rites of passage into adulthood.

Q: Can you describe how some mothers have double standards for their sons and daughters and how we can do a better job teaching Black boys to be responsible?

A: I have a theory that some mothers raise their daughters and love their sons. It is of utmost concern to me when parents are more effective with their daughters than their sons. These mothers will teach their daughters how to cook, sew, clean, and wash dishes, and will make them come home early to study. They will also make their daughters go to church and mandate their involvement in constructive programs for their growth and development. On the other hand they do not teach their sons how to cook, sew, clean, and wash dishes. Many mothers make it optional for their sons to attend church, sing in the choir, and attend tutorial sessions. This has become a real concern because they know how to be effective parents, as demonstrated with the way they treat their daughters.

Then there are the mothers who tell their nine-year-old sons, "You're the man of the house." Yet, as I mentioned previously, manhood is earned and not given. I don't believe a nine-year-old boy is ready to be the man of the house. If an 18-year-old boy is not working but he wants a hundred dollar pair of shoes, the likelihood will be that his mother will buy them. We have 40-year-old "boys" still living at home with their mothers. He can't do without her and she can't do without him. We have a lot of mama's boys and it needs to be curtailed.

There are many reasons why some mothers raise their daughters and love their sons. Historically it originated with large numbers of African American males being lynched and castrated. There are a lot of unconscious reasons why we do it today. Some mothers simply behave based on what they observed when they were children. Their mothers did not make their brothers do much domestic work. They allowed their brothers to rip and run the streets. Some wives have husbands who do not do housework and don't want their sons to either. Another reason we've heard some mothers give is they're afraid that if their sons do household work they may be labeled "sissies." This fear is homophobic. My concern is that if Black women are so well versed about what Black men do and do not do, they should realize their little boy is someone's future husband and father, and all the problems and flaws they noticed in their own husband should be corrected with their sons.

One reason for this situation may be rooted in the mother's own problems with her ex-husband. Subconsciously, she wants her son to remain a child, dependent on her and a continual reminder of her failed marriage. We have mothers who in a very negative way tell their sons, "You're going to be just like your daddy." Our position is that if you have a problem with your ex-husband, that's between you and him, not your son. The situation between the mother and son in the film "The Women of Brewster Place" is a glaring example of how some mothers and sons become destructively connected to each other.

A consequence of this double standard is teenage pregnancy, which has reached epidemic proportions with 75% of our youth being born out of wedlock. Although most people recognize the need to address this problem, 90% of the pregnancy prevention programs only counsel females. We make statements like, "Boys will be boys," and yes, they will if you allow them to be. We must teach responsibility at a very early age. It's ineffective to start at sixteen when youth have already made babies. We should start very early and encourage the development of responsibility about personal hygiene, clothes, room upkeep, chores, toys and equipment, earning an allowance, studying, and then sexuality.

SELF-ESTEEM

Q: How important is identity in the growth and development of our children?

A: It is the most important factor. On many Egyptian pyramids, temples, and tombs are the words, "Know Thyself." Until people know whose they are, God's child, and who they are, African or African-American, they will continue to exist in the wilderness. Oppressed people don't realize the value of identity. It was only when "Detroit Red" (Malcolm X) knew *whose* he was, and *who* he was, that he could then take his rightful place in the world.

Abraham Lincoln figured out that if a plantation has 300 slaves and one master, it will require a lot of effort to oversee all those slaves. But if you let the slaves go, don't teach them identity, and don't make them feel good about themselves, you won't have to watch them. They will rape, rob, and steal from each other. There are no more chains around their wrists and ankles; now it's a matter of placing chains around their minds. Whoever controls the mind will also control the body. Whoever controls the identity of a people will also determine their destiny. Identity is the most important factor.

Many people like to compare African-Americans to Asians, Jews, and our brothers and sisters from the West Indies. African-Americans constitute one category and the other three groups comprise another category. When these two categories are compared, people like to say all four groups have been oppressed, but the second category of people is doing a much better job of succeeding in the United States. The problem with this comparison, though, is that we're comparing immigrants to slaves. A group which voluntarily came here can't be compared to a group forced to be here. Nevertheless, we can learn from people who make the comparison argument, because the three groups of people in the second category have their culture intact. It is the invisible ingredient that most affects one's identity. Research by Harold Cruse shows anyone who leaves a known place and goes to an unknown place has a strong sense of identity, self-esteem, work ethic, and entrepreneurial spirit. The present power structure is very much aware of the importance of self-esteem.

The problem is, how can you expect victims who have never been taught their history, or have only been taught it in February, or have only been given a docile approach to their history, to realize its importance? Most Black people end up saying, "I don't want to hear none of that black stuff." I don't get frustrated anymore when I hear that response because I understand I'm talking to a victim.

Q: How significant is the term "African-American?"

A: My first comment is that the term did not originate with Jesse Jackson. I respect Jesse but it amazes me how the media take something and run with it. People like Paul Cuffe, Martin Delaney, Richard Allen and many other unsung men and women of our past knew they were African as far back as 200 years before Jesse. Those men and women used the terms African or African-American for a long time. Jesse Jackson did not discover the name — the media discovered Jesse. We have been called all kinds of names: colored, Negro, Black, Afro-American, African, American, and African-American.

Alex Haley, in the book and movie "Roots," points out that Germans are Germans because there's a land called Germany, and the Chinese are Chinese because of a land called China. I think land is a good criteria for the name we choose. There's no place in the world called Negro, Color, Black, or Afro-America. You can be born anywhere but your roots remain the same. There are only two appropriate answers left, African and American. So if someone asks you where you were born, you were born in

America. And if someone asks you who you are and where your roots are, your roots are in Africa; that's how you come up with the name African-American.

What's interesting about this issue of names is that before we came to America we called ourselves African. On the slave ship we were supposed to call ourselves colored. Around 1860 a large number of us began to call ourselves Negro. In those days, calling someone Black was an insult. During the 1960s we became comfortable with the word "Black." Then in the 1970s many of us called ourselves Afro-American. The 1980s saw a large number of us calling ourselves African-American, and maybe at some future point we'll return to calling ourselves African — born in many places in the world but remaining African.

I've watched numerous talk shows and been on many of them where people whom I respect — such as business people and older folks who are highly skilled and very active in our communities — are somewhat annoyed about this question. They feel that with all the problems we face — including drugs, AIDS, adolescent pregnancy, unemployment, and low academic achievement — we don't need to get hung up on this issue. I disagree; I think we need to address everything. We can establish who we are and that can assist us in solving a myriad of problems. This does not have to become an either/or issue, but I respect those people who'd rather allocate 100% of their time dealing with some other concerns than looking at what we call ourselves.

I do think identity is important, though. When we look at historical incidents such as the Montgomery bus boycott, where for 381 days we established our own temporary "bus company," the lack of identity became a factor. When Whites finally realized we were serious about discrimination and they were losing money because of the boycott, they wanted us to return to using the city buses. But if we had understood what freedom and identity really meant and stopped defining freedom as being liked by other people, we would have seen ourselves as a people who are producers and owners, not just consumers who are loyal to other people who know their identity. We would have said freedom for us does not mean riding your buses or living in your houses, but establishing our own. I think identity is important, but I respect those who are at least trying to do something for the liberation of our people.

Many people are afraid the media will give more attention to the name we call ourselves and not deal with issues like how to counter the conspiracy to destroy Black boys.

Q: Can you explain exactly what is good hair and pretty eyes?

A: Many people are brainwashed into thinking that good hair is long, straight and blond, and pretty eyes are blue, green, or hazel. Based on this Euro-centric definition, large numbers of African-Americans do not have good hair and pretty eyes. This concept originated when White slave masters could not keep their hands off our women and they created mulatto offspring. Often the masters had their light-skinned offspring work in the house while the dark-skinned slaves worked in the fields. That situation fostered a great degree of tension and animosity which continues to persist.

Not very long ago, many Black colleges required a photograph to be submitted with a student's application and those who were of a darker hue were not admitted to the school. I believe we'll be free when we no longer associate good hair and pretty eyes with European features. Frances Welsing said that your brain is your computer and everything you've seen is stored there. We need to reprogram our "computers" and look at dark-skinned African-American people long and hard until we convince ourselves that we're beautiful just the way we are. Your hair is good because it's "wash and wear" hair in its natural state. You can swim, sweat, and do anything you want and your hair will still be "good."

Black women also need to be aware that White women do not jump out of a pool and go straight to the prom. They wash their hair daily, blow-dry it, and spend a lot of time with their hair; African women simply do not have to go to a hairdresser once or every other week to make their hair look attractive. I think we also need to realize the benefits of dark skin. Because of the composition of dark skin, it has less chance of sunburn and skin cancer, and it delays the aging process. The skin of two 70-year-old women — one Black and one White — does not look the same. We need to realize the darker you are the more melanin you have, and the more melanin you have the more sun you can absorb. The more you can absorb sunlight, the greater amount of vitamin D you produce, and the more you produce vitamin D the greater the chance for brain cell development. It's very interesting that Europeans want to convince us of our inferiority based on our skin color, yet they spend long vacation hours in the sun trying to get a suntan.

Q: How significantly do images and words influence self-esteem?

A: Images and words are very powerful, and the power brokers of the world figured it was much easier to take the chains off the wrists and ankles and put the chains around the mind. Images and words are our contemporary chains. When you hear the words BLACK and WHITE in an insecure country like America and other countries where racism exists, those words are used as diabolical opposites. Black is used in a negative way and white is used in a positive manner. When you look up the word "black" in a thesaurus you find over 200 negative connotations, but when you look up the word "white" you find several positive characteristics.

Everyday examples abound. When you hear the word "black," you'll hear "black nigger," "black sheep of the family," "I'm gonna blackball you," "I'll put you on the black list," "behind the eight ball" (which is black), "devil's food cake" (which is chocolate), and "the dark continent." Those things are associated with the word "black" and they're all negative in some way. The word "white" is associated with "good" things. There's "angel food cake" (which is white), weddings with a white dress, gloves, and hat (to symbolize the bride's purity), Superman, Santa Claus, and even Jesus Christ are all portrayed as white men. Jesus Christ is probably the most powerful image of all.

Only insecure people would need to place God in their own image. We should worship Him in spirit and truth, but if we must portray His image we should at least picture Him in the way He came to earth. He came here as an African. How do we know? He had hair the texture of wool and feet the color of bronze, as reported in the Bible in the Books of Daniel and Revelation. He came from the line of David, who was Hamitic, and the Hamitic people are Black. He was born on the continent of Africa. But in 1505 Pope Julius II commissioned Michaelangelo to paint Jesus as a White man in spite of the presence of seven to eight Shrines of the Black Madonna around the world, including one in Poland which the current pope continues to worship. Not only was Jesus Black but His mother Mary was as well.

Images are extremely powerful and that's why I also mentioned Santa Claus and Superman. The 1954 Clark study and one conducted in 1988 still show Black children choose dolls that are either lighter-skinned than them or white-skinned before they choose dolls of their own skin color. There are several reasons for this. One of them is related to the complexity of studies like these. You can't separate what a child's been exposed to from the decisions they make about items like toys and dolls. Many times White manufacturers do not produce attractive Black dolls. They have dipped "Ken" and "Barbie" into black paint and our children do not want that kind of doll. We commend those Black manufacturers who are producing dolls dressed in African attire, with African features; this reinforces our culture. Until we increase the number, variety, quality, and visibility of Black dolls in the stores, our children will continue to choose dolls that do not look like them.

Q: Can an African-American have self-esteem without racial pride?

A: Yes, it's possible to have strong self-esteem without racial pride. There are children who are very strong-willed and have extremely accomplished parents who've been able to transmit pride to them. There are students who are high achievers in academics, sports, or music, and that has been a source of their self-esteem. Then there are children who will tell you, "I'm just going to be me." In my book *To be Popular or Smart: The Black Peer Group,* I mentioned this phenomenon is called being "raceless." Raceless people do not identify with being Black or White and are uncomfortable with either one. They sincerely believe they can go through life just being themselves.

Unfortunately, they are still viewed, whether they like it or not, as being a member of the African community and at some point they'll be strongly reminded of their racial origin. Overall, I feel it's better to be reminded by your own community rather than from the outside, and to secure the strength of your community instead of receiving the brunt of institutional racism later on. It's really disheartening to see 25-year-old men and women who have attended prestigious universities, obtained lots of academic degrees, who now work in corporate America and sincerely believe they will be chief executive officers or vice presidents — only to discover there's a ceiling in that corporation beyond which they cannot be promoted. They may have to train someone — who does not look like them and who has fewer degrees and qualifications — to be their supervisor.

Yes, there are children operating under the assumption that they can just be themselves. They're allowed to proceed to some degree with that notion, but racism at some point will remind them they're African in White America. John Johnson, owner of Johnson Publishing Company, one of the richest Africans in the world and among the 400 top corporate leaders of all the world's races, offers many incidents in his life during which he has still been viewed as less than a man. Johnson's strength comes from never forgetting his Arkansas upbringing. The problem with many people is that they try to forget.

Q: Are there other forms of esteem besides self-esteem, and what are the major factors that contribute to strong self-esteem?

A: Many different forms of esteem exist besides self-esteem. There are peer, parent, spouse, career, material, and physical esteem, just to name a few. For example, physical esteem results when people do not feel good about themselves or their self-worth (which is a synonym of self-esteem). Their self-worth is dependent upon their physical health and how they look, especially their weight. Many people's esteem is affected because of their weight. If they gain 25 or 30 pounds their esteem is often lowered. They are not comfortable with the way they look if they are not physically fit or their health is poor. If they are suffering from a disease or illness, that can also affect their self-esteem. For many of us, our esteem is based on our physical health, diet, and weight.

For others, esteem is based on material possessions. For many of us, our self-worth is based on the car we drive or the clothes we wear. Many of us cannot quit our jobs tomorrow. We make $20,000 and we spend $20,000 or more. In low income areas you'll often notice there are finer cars parked near the projects than there are in affluent suburbs. There are secretaries who work downtown and make under $10,000; they outdress their bosses who make over $60,000. These people measure their worth by their possessions.

Others of us trace our esteem to other sources. Some of us base our esteem on our careers, jobs, and degrees. We say, "I've got a B.A., an M.A., and a Ph.D. I'm vice president in charge of the closets. I'm in charge of you, you, and you." It sort of reminds me of the Head Negro in Charge, the HNIC. Others of us base our esteem on our spouses—no man, no esteem, no woman, no esteem. One of every two husbands physically abuses his wife at some point. Many people think the problem is only with the man who does the beating, but I believe there's more to it than that. I believe that any respectable woman makes it very clear to her man, "If you put a hand on me, either I'm leaving or you'd better not go to sleep."

There are two kinds of women in America; let's say they go by the names of Donna and Kathy. Donna feels very good about herself. She would like to have a man but she doesn't. The sun will still shine and God will still be first in her life. Then there's Kathy, who will take him any way he comes through the door—with another woman, a bottle, or a balled-up fist. Kathy just wants a man and half a man will do. There are many women and some men who base their esteem on their spouse. If they have no mate, they have no esteem.

Now let's discuss parent esteem. There are many parents who live their lives through their children, and there are many adults who are still trying to please their parents. It is very difficult to feel good about yourself when you're still trying to please someone else. In 1923 Kahlil Gibran wrote a book titled *The Prophet* which described parents who want to live their lives through their children. We also want parents to realize the effects of what they say to their children. Often, we only look at physical abuse. One study looking at parents' statements found that of the 314 statements made to children, 296 of them were negative. The negative statements included, "Don't do this and don't do that," "You idiot," "Sit your ___ ___ ___ down," and "Keep your mouth shut."

I'm very concerned about incidents in which I'm out in public and I see parents who I know love their children but say damaging things to them. Many children have excellent memories. If you tell them at an early age that they are idiots, imbeciles, stupid, or they should keep their mouths shut, they will replay those conversations in their heads. I believe these parents love their children; they hug them, and they buy them candy and everything else in the store after they've just made these kind of statements. I would rather they not buy their children things and avoid these statements, because you can't replace verbal abuse with a candy bar. We have to be very careful with parent esteem. Kahlil Gibran reminds us, "your children do not belong to you, they belong to God."

Then there's peer esteem. We all realize how powerfully peer pressure affects our children. In 1950 and 1980 the University of Michigan conducted a study looking at various influences on children. The study was repeated in 1989 by a professor at Wayne State University. Listed below are their findings:

1950	1980	1989
home	home	peer
school	peer	television/radio
church	television	home
peer	school	school
television	church	church

Peer pressure is a very significant issue and good parents have found ways to monitor peer pressure. First, these parents know who their children's friends are. Second, they invite their children's friends over so they can get to know them better. Third, they program their children's peer group by placing them in programs that reinforce the parents' value system. Last but not least, they have their children regularly contact them so they can keep tabs on their children's activities.

There are children who leave home in the morning and are not seen or heard from until 8, 9, or 10:00 in the evening. Good parents maintain contact with their children, sometimes on an hourly basis. I'm not saying a child can't deal drugs or get pregnant in an hour, but when a child has to check back with his parents on the hour, it makes unproductive behavior more difficult. In my book, *To be Popular or Smart: The Black Peer Group*, we discuss this issue in more detail. One of our major concerns is that it's very possible for parents and teachers to be doing their jobs, and it can all be for naught because the Black peer group is more concerned with the kind of gym shoes and clothes they wear, and how well they dance, fight, and play basketball. The Black peer group is not currently reinforcing academic achievement and we must find ways to infiltrate it and reinforce scholastic achievement.

The most important esteem is self-esteem — not peer, parent, spouse, career, material, or physical. Self-esteem is really difficult for both children and adults to acquire. I think the factors that best contribute to developing self-esteem are: your relationship with God, unconditional love from parents, high expectations from teachers, feeling good about your race, identifying your talents and previous accomplishments, and for young people college plans or career goals. The more of these factors that you have working for you, the greater chance you'll have self-esteem. As I mentioned in response to the previous question, a child can have self-esteem without the racial component because any one of the seven factors can contribute to self-esteem. But the more of these factors you have working for you, I believe your self-esteem will be stabler and more secure. The best contributor to self-esteem is your relationship with God.

Q: What is the relationship between self-esteem and academic achievement?

A: Numerous studies show that children who have strong self-esteem also do well in school. That's very hard to indicate quantitatively, because it's difficult to quantify self-esteem. Children who give good eye contact, communicate with adults, are confident, and try hard, perform better academically. It's difficult to say, for instance, that when self-esteem increases 3.5% that ACT scores rise 2.7%, but few educators deny a relationship between self-esteem and academic achievement.

At African-American Images we have designed a manual called SETCLAE (Self-Esteem Through Culture Leads to Academic Excellence). We work with school districts and examine three variables: self-esteem, culture, and academic excellence. We give participating children a pre-test in self-esteem, provide teachers with lesson plans from a cultural perspective to strengthen self-esteem, and upon completion of the curriculum, we conduct a post-test. SETCLAE can be integrated into the existing language arts or social studies curriculum, or it can be taught as a separate unit. I feel there's a direct, positive relationship between self-esteem and academic achievement, and we are attempting to improve self-esteem through SETCLAE.

MOTIVATION

Q: How do you motivate Black youth?

A: From a psychological perspective, motivation comes either from within or from the outside. Motivation from outside a person usually emerges as a result of some external factor, a "carrot" that is presented to the person to motivate him or her. I noticed your question, "How do you motivate Black youth?" did not include, to do what? All youth are motivated. They may not be motivated in academics, but many are extremely motivated to wear designer clothes, drive fancy cars, play in the NBA, and be the latest rap star. The "carrots" for many of our youth are clothes, automobiles, sports, and music careers.

We've got to find more academic "carrots" that also stimulate children. External motivation cannot be separated from role models. It's very difficult to be an engineer if you have never seen one. Our children need more positive Black role models to interest them in achieving academically. They see many more role models in sports and music than they do in math and science. Interestingly, I was once in New York City and a teacher said the children in her class were not motivated in mathematics; however, they did extremely well in the metric section of the curriculum. She didn't understand that they did so well in metrics because they were motivated—they could identify with kilos, grams, and other metric measurements due to the drug industry's use of metrics. Schools need to glorify academic achievement the way they do with athletic achievement. We must also help youth find the God-given talents so they can increase their internal motivation.

Q: Why does there appear to be a decline in motivation to learn in the classroom as age increases?

A: There are two major reasons. As your question implies, when children first come into the classroom they are highly motivated to learn and be involved in the process. We must acknowledge that children come to us motivated. Something we do turns them off. I think we need to honestly look at the fact that as children's ages increase their questions decrease. It is very difficult to learn if you're not involved in the process. In his book, *Pedagogy of the Oppressed,* Paulo Freire describes what he calls the "banking approach." A teacher looks at students as receptacles, who are only there for the teacher to deposit information. There is little dialogue and interaction—that's not education. When they first come to school, children naively think they will be involved in the process and they will learn things related to their world. They also think they have a right to ask why they are learning. But very early in the school year, children discover that their questions are not as significant as the predetermined subject areas to be taught, and to question how this process relates to their own world would be insubordinate. So after a while they no longer ask questions and their motivation declines. They find other ways to stimulate themselves, in the classroom or on the streets. Children begin to realize, then, that school is about grades not learning; consequently, the older they become the more they cheat.

Peer pressure also increases as age increases and this tends to decrease a child's motivation to learn. Unfortunately, the Black peer group has taken the position that to be smart is to be White. This point of view shows that many Black youth are more confident in sports and music than they are in math, science, and language arts; and rather than confronting their fear, they conveniently avoid it and attribute studious behavior to being White. If you're on record as saying that being smart is being White, then if you aren't smart, you're okay because you wanted to be Black in the first place.

Q: How do you get youth to value long-term gratification over short-term gratification?

A: This is one of the most difficult questions I've ever had to answer. I recently encountered a youth who's about 19 years old, and he told me point-blank that he would rather die at 21 years of age and have at least two years of driving a BMW—even if it means he'd have to sell drugs—than live 65 years with a slave job or no job, and never own a car. He told me I made very good sense, he understood my positions about valuing life and living for the long term, and he acknowledged that there might be a possibility he could do well and have a successful career. But with all things considered, he had better odds of owning a BMW by selling drugs than with an education. He said he didn't mind the prospect of dying in two years if he could be rich for a couple of years.

My first response to this question is that I don't think anyone likes working 24 hours if given the option of working one. I don't think children ever prefer waiting a year for a bicycle versus waiting a day. We know in child development that if a child is five years old and you tell the child to wait a year that seems like a lifetime to the child, because that's 20% of the life the child has lived. For an adult who may be 40 years old, one year is simply 1/40 of his or her life. I think adults need to appreciate that children, being younger, have a different view of the world — if for no other reason than they've been in it for a shorter period of time than adults.

Nowadays, the question of motivation as it relates to academic achievement has a different twist. When you ask our children what their parents tell them they should want out of life, they'll probably say they should get a good education and work hard. However, our children are asking questions such as, "Work hard for whom?" and "Get a good education for what?" They do not want to be employees, they want to be employers. They have no desire to end up on welfare or work in McDonald's. Children watch adults who have a good education, working a JOB. If all a JOB brought was TGIF (money), our children have found five other ways to make money that don't require a good education or great effort in the classroom. This also competes with children's attention and interest in the short term. Our children feel they can make more money and make it faster in drugs, non-drug-related crime, sports, music, and the lottery; those five areas have become our competition.

We have to show children there are better odds in the academic arena than there are in drugs, sports, crime, music, and the lottery. For example, our children see drug winners but rarely do they see drug losers. We need to take them to prisons, drug abuse programs, hospitals, and cemeteries. We must have them write a list of all the people they know who have been selling drugs for five years and report their current status. We must show them the mathematical odds, listed below, of making it in the NBA:

1,000,000 (wanted Michael Jordan's job)
400,000 (made the high school team)
4,000 (made the college team)
35 (got on an NBA team)
7 (started)
4 (years of an average career)

Often times I give young people six options, and I ask them which one they would choose:

car — Porsche
clothes — all you can wear
mansion — 30 bedrooms
land — 100,000 acres
money — one million dollars
time

The brothers in the group often choose the car as their first choice, and many sisters choose clothes as their number one selection. Many adults choose the mansion first. Others choose money as their first option, but then I tease them and ask what they would do with the money and they say they would buy a car, clothes and a house; so we're back to the first three options. Better students choose land. This means they understand what's on their back comes from land, and money can be made in a factory. Land is the most important resource in the world, but there is one that's even more important — TIME. When you leave this earth, you will leave with the car in the garage, clothes in the closet, a house on the block, and money in the bank. But you will leave with no more time. It's our most precious resource. If you believe in short-term gratification, there's a very good chance that, like the

19-year-old brother who doesn't mind dying at age 21, you'll miss your most important resource and the one you can't recapture — time.

I think it's also important for our children to observe or read about wealthy people and notice that in many cases they are not happy. Children also need to talk to people who are in the Lord. The peace the Lord can give you far exceeds any feeling you get from owning cars, clothes, and a mansion. This does not mean that when you're working toward getting a B.A. or M.A., you shouldn't enjoy short-term victories or rewards. It's nice along the way to receive trophies or treat yourself to nice things. Long-term gratification does not mean that you starve for years before you begin to enjoy the good life. There can be short-term victories. I think we as adults need to provide them to our youth at regular intervals, to encourage them to resist the onslaught of materialism currently being experienced by their drug dealing peers.

Q: What does a teacher do when a child does not do the work in class and does not turn in homework assignments, and the parents are uncooperative? What can we do to motivate the child to do school work?

A: I would recommend a number of different strategies. Concerning uncooperative parents, first we need to develop a case history of the family to find out what is causing this hindrance. Most parents want to do what's best for the child, even though we do have parents who unequivocally side with the child, come up to the school, and curse out the teacher. Secondly, I think we need to also interact with parents about positive situations. We shouldn't just call when there are problems with a child; we should also contact parents when good things happen. Many parents get nervous when they hear from their child's school. In addition, I recommend that parents also reinforce positive behavior from their child and praise the child's teacher for doing the job well. Unfortunately, we do a better job of reinforcing the negative over the positive. I would also recommend cooperative learning. A child who does not do homework could be motivated with positive peer pressure. If the child belonged to an academic team whose overall score would be affected by individual negligence, I'm confident the team would motivate the youth to a better performance level.

Q: How do we get youth as motivated in academics as they appear to be in sports and music?

A: Our children are responsive to sports and music for many reasons. Money and glory are two of them. This overexaggeration on wealth and popularity originates primarily with the media and the three professional sports, but it also comes from schools that give more glory to athletes than scholars. Where are the pep rallies for the honor-roll students? Where are the medals, trophies, and awards ceremonies for the debate, spelling, and science competition winners? Schools give big trophies to their athletes and mass printed certificates to scholars. I think schools are giving a very clear message to children about how much they value academic achievement.

We also need to give our children a realistic picture of their chances of going to the NBA, NFL, or playing major league baseball. A million brothers want these jobs, but only 7 will make it to professional sports and the average career lasts four years. The average career in music is five years in duration. One of the factors involved here is that sports and music seem so enjoyable. Our classrooms could be more enjoyable and allow more physical movement. I challenge teachers to allow children to move around the room, place them on academic teams, and give them significant awards for academic achievement. I think we would see a very exciting development in our youth.

Q: What is the relationship between peer pressure and motivation?

A: There is a direct relationship between the two. For many of our students, peer pressure is now in the number one position in their lives. Unfortunately, many Black youth associate being smart with being White. Our children are very confident in sports and music, but they don't seem to be confident in academics; and rather than confronting their fear, many have decided to avoid it by simply associating academic pursuits with being White. It is very possible for parents and teachers to do their jobs and it all goes for naught because the Black peer group is more concerned about such social issues as designer clothes, rap records, and dating than academic achievement. We've got to infiltrate the Black peer group to reprogram our youth so they will associate being smart with being Black.

Q: How can we reduce the dropout rate?

A: We can reduce the dropout rate by increasing teacher expectations and parental involvement, eliminating tracking, improving self-esteem, developing a relevant curriculum with appropriate methodologies for Black children's learning styles, and structuring positive peer pressure through cooperative learning. We not only can reduce the dropout rate, but these strategies can also maximize academic achievement. In lieu of the fact that many times these areas are not addressed satisfactorily, we advocate an intervention team which will help youth starting at the fourth grade. Studies show that youth who are below their grade level in academic achievement are prime targets to become dropouts. The intervention team can reduce the number of youth falling behind academically.

Additionally, if we expose our boys to positive role models this may also turn them around. Furthermore, if we establish a partnership between businesses and schools, employers can provide scholarships and employment opportunities for students.

Q: What is the impact of high unemployment and drugs on academic motivation?

A: The impact is severe and has sapped the motivation of many of our youth to pursue academics. Many of our youth wonder why they should study if there are no jobs down the road. I've always been amazed by the white middle class and specifically White males who talk about the lack of motivation among Black youth, when everyone knows a White boy with a high school diploma will make more money than anyone of color with a college degree. It's difficult to talk about someone's lack of motivation when there are so many cards stacked against Black youth. The unemployment rate among Black youth is 50% or more and it's 25-30% among Black adults. Many Black adults who are working are paid the minimum wage and that's also detrimental to youth's motivation. The issue becomes even more complicated when children not only don't see the need to get a high school diploma or seek legitimate employment, they're also aware they can sell drugs and make more money in one day than many college educated people make in a year.

The unemployment and drug problems have been catastrophic. I want to stress that the best way to deal with the drug question is to show our children drug losers, because they seem to be mesmerized by the drug winners they observe. We have to show them there are better odds in the classroom than selling drugs.

I believe you can't be a leader in our community without an agenda on drugs. No decision is a decision. I suggest six responses to the issue of drugs. First, I recommend placing more pressure on the federal government to prevent the flow of drugs coming in at the nation's borders. The U. S. government knows that 85% of all illicit drugs comes through southern Florida. Yet the government cut the Coast Guard's budget by one hundred million dollars. The drug industry has exceeded the car industry in sales volume. Many banks would go broke without drug-related money. My second suggestion—and none of these ideas is exclusive of each other—would be to reinforce strong self-esteem within our youth. When Malcolm X learned *whose* he was and *who* he was, drugs were no longer an influence in his life. We must give our young people something to lose, something they value so much they would not make the mistake of drug involvement. "Just say no" is not enough; our youth need something to say yes to. I know of no better source of esteem than God, the race, and youth themselves. Thirdly, we should allow no stores in our communities to sell drug paraphernalia. We must first make our concerns known to store owners, and if they don't remove the items, we should boycott those stores. I respect the fine efforts of Fathers Clements and Pfleger, Dick Gregory, and so many others who have pressured stores that sell drug-related products to our children.

Fourth, I advocate that when the police make a bust the monies should go to the community that has been devastated by drugs, rather than to the police that often are in on the take. Legislation should be developed at the local, state, and national levels to make this suggestion a reality. Fifth, we need more men to emulate the fine example of the Nation of Islam's Dopebuster program. I think it's ironic that William Bennett the Drug Czar wanted to spend 70 million dollars in Washington, D.C.— primarily to build more prisons that do not work—but did not want to replicate the Dopebuster program, which is already in use in Washington and is effective and free. We need Christian men who will stand with Muslim men and tell our youth and older drug dealers, "You will not sell drugs in our communities."

Lastly, and I definitely mean this as a last resort, we should consider the legalization of drugs. Kurt Schmoke, mayor of Baltimore, is among those who have suggested this option in part because they are very much aware that the penal system has failed to arrest the drug problem. Sixty percent of America's inmates are in jail because of drug-related crimes. It is impossible to build prisons quickly enough to house the growing number of those convicted for drug crimes. Many law-abiding citizens are afraid to be out in the evening, and burglar alarms are common additions to cars and homes because most crime is drug related. Schmoke and others realize that many of our youth don't study or attend school because of the high profits available through drug sales. The legalization of drugs would remove the profit motive.

The other problem of course is drug addiction. Can you imagine buying crack at a pharmacy? We lost 6,000 people to hard drugs in 1988, 100,000 to alcohol, and 300,000 to nicotine and caffeine. The number lost to hard drugs would shoot up astronomically if these substances were legalized, but the public would be safer, prisons would be less crowded, and more youth would rely on education instead of drugs to secure prosperity. I ask those people against Mayor Schmoke's suggestion, what is your suggestion? Remember, no decision is a decision. What is your agenda on the drug issue?

In terms of the impact of high unemployment on academic achievement, we must pressure the government to fund job-training programs and create more jobs. We must also pressure ourselves to create jobs. If every member of the Black middle class would create one job for Black youth, many of these problems would be resolved. I believe in a two-pronged approach to the economic and unemployment question, in which both the government and self-determination provide the solutions.

ADMINISTRATION

Q: What do you look for in a good superintendent?

A: The superintendent is the overall leader of a school district and this person must be very clear about his or her objectives. The superintendent cannot approach the job with an acceptance of the status quo. He or she needs to clearly articulate to everyone his or her views on various issues related to education. The superintendent should have good networking skills to establish a relationship with the school board, unions, and businesses. The superintendent has to make people who are protecting mediocrity feel uncomfortable and outmoded. He or she has to have thick skin and not be in the job for the purpose of being liked. The superintendent must have the best interests of the child as the top priority.

A slogan often used in education is, "what's good for the children," but it appears that school boards, unions, and local businesses have other priorities. Superintendents should be evaluated on whether their decisions were made for the sake of the children. The problem is, boards appoint superintendents, not children. Their future is dependent on as few as two or three votes, and many board members — when they are elected — have obtained their positions with very few votes from the community because of low voter turnout. A good superintendent will not compromise children's needs, epsecially if the board has a value system that opposes those needs.

A very good friend of mine who is the superintendent of a large school district understood very clearly that the first thing he had to do was to hold teachers accountable and identify the lowest achieving school in the district. He knew he could not have bad teachers fired because of union regulations. So he asked that all teachers at this school be transferred and then he solicited very good teachers from around the district to teach at the lowest achieving school. My friend stated clearly that in his first year as superintendent the problem was never with the children, but with low teacher expectations. To me that is the kind of leadership we need in a school district. If I were a superintendent, I would first identify low achieving schools and try to reallocate my staff to deal with issues like teacher expectations.

The next area I would attack would be tracking. I would abolish tracking and divide children into either heterogenous, cooperative learning, or learning style groups. Thirdly, I would overhaul the curriculum and make it more culturally relevant. The fourth measure I would undertake would be to secure support from the business community for summer youth employment, scholarships, and awards for academic achievement. I would also try to reduce the number of administrative positions at the district level by either removing them completely or placing them within local schools. Lastly, I would make sure we increase the number of contracts awarded to African American businesses. Miseducation continues, but White-owned businesses still profit from it. I would institute competitive bidding, reduce administrative costs, and channel the monies into the classroom with more staff.

Q: What do you look for in a good principal?

A: The principal's job is a very challenging one because it is actually two jobs. There is the management function which involves running the building and all its resources, and there's also the instructional component which requires an understanding of instruction and evaluation. Inherent in management and instruction is motivating students and staff and making sure the school is safe. If I had to rank all these areas, I would say a principal is the instructional leader of a school. This person should not be running around with a baseball bat and a bullhorn, beating up students. Schools need to be safe, but there may be someone else in the school who can provide that function. We can also make a school safe without turning it into a prison.

In my opinion, good principals arrive early or stay late to take care of the the paperwork — the management end of being a principal — but during the school day they are the instructional leaders of schools. They understand instruction and evaluation. They regularly observe teachers and they know the students. For that reason they are able to improve and sustain academic achievement in the classroom.

I expect strong leadership in a principal and while that's a nice code phrase, strong leadership can be expressed in a number of ways. One way is by making it uncomfortable for teachers to remain if they don't have high expectations of their students. Another expression of strong leadership occurs through in-service training. I have spoken at numerous schools where the principal made the meeting optional. The teachers who attended were already interested in the ideas I was going to present. In many cases, they were already pursuing those techniques and the workshop was really a reinforcement. I believe in-service meetings like those should be mandatory. It may be hard on me as a consultant to speak to people who do not want to hear my ideas, but I think it's more effective for the overall growth and development of our children and that's why I'm there.

A principal should also develop a relationship with his or her staff that is mutually reinforcing and motivating. Principals have a very demanding position; they must respect their staff and be fair. But the respect should be mutual and should reinforce a team-oriented approach to education. I have been in schools where this approach exists; there is a family-like atmosphere and the principal had clearly established the school's goals. Each person understood his or her function, they respected each other and worked as a team. In many low achieving schools this kind of environment is not present and there's tension among everyone. I've observed schools where the principal and teachers ate lunch together and shared their experiences with each other. These principals are fair with teachers. On the other hand, there are principals who operate with the attitude, "If I like you, you'll get various benefits and if I don't like you, negative things will happen." That's not the way good principals operate. They proceed on the principle of fairness. If you look at sports teams, you'll notice the better teams don't always have the best talent; good coaches bring out the best from their players. Good principals do the same with their staff. Some principals have received a lot of media attention, but they have an antagonistic relationship with their staff and they are not the instructional leaders of their schools.

Q: Describe the "Effective Schools Project" as it relates to administrators.

A: The five major elements of the "Effective Schools Project" are: strong leadership, high teacher expectations, increased time on task, a positive school climate, and clearly understood goals and objectives for instruction and precise reporting mechanisms for evaluation. A principal within the context of the "Effective Schools Project" would not only be the instructional leader but would also establish a positive school climate. Schools need to be safe and other principals—who receive little media attention —have done this with few if any bullhorns, bats, metal detectors, and security guards. A secure environment was maintained by instilling school pride, enhancing self-esteem and giving students, parents, and teachers a sense of ownership.

Principals participating in the "Effective Schools Project" must also deal with time on task. I know some effective schools where a designated period, from 9:00-11:00 a.m., is reading time and absolutely no interruptions are allowed. This is the prime time of the school day and these principals want to make sure they maximize it. They have determined that time on task is very significant and will do whatever they can to prevent interruptions to their teachers.

Q: The research from Ron Edmonds and the Effective Schools Project places its total emphasis on the school to improve academic achievement. What do you think about the research coming from James Comer which posits that administrators need to reach out to parents, teachers, and the community in order to be effective?

A: The School Development program, administered by the Yale Child Study Center and headed by James Comer, has been very effective in New Haven and other cities of similar size. James Comer believes that many problems in the schools are not related so much to academic as to relationship issues. These include lack of respect, discipline, motivation, teacher attitude, and poor parental involvement. Comer asserts that the root of these problems lies in the adversarial nature of the relations between schools and homes in many low-income areas. To address this, a team-oriented approach was devised which gives parents, teachers, and the community more authority. The program's premise was based on the notion that when parents felt welcomed and participated in meaningful ways, they would reinforce academic achievement at home. Each school has an administrative and mental health team which implements and monitors the program. I support the program, but I want to reiterate that it has been successful in smaller cities where it's easier to monitor. Larger cities are questioning whether the program can be as effective in a broader context. As an administrator with limited resources of time and money, I would invest in the Edmonds approach first because we control the hours of 9:00 until 3:00 and when we have done our job satisfactorily, we'll pursue Comer's model.

PARENTING

Q: How can the school and the home have a closer relationship?

A: I think we can learn from the successes of Headstart, Chapter I, and the School Development Program. These three programs mandate parental involvement and they sincerely want to interact with parents. Each program has a paid parent coordinator, a parent room on site, and the programs are designed to assist in parents' development. These programs fully understand that children will develop much faster and more productively when the parents not only are involved with their children, but are growing and developing themselves. Elementary and high schools will have to honestly ask themselves if they really want to improve parent-school relationships. If they do, the major area that needs to be revised is communication.

Very little communication exists between home and school; when communication occurs, it's usually problematic. We need communication between home and school that includes times when children do well. We need schools to ask themselves what they really want parents to do. Do they want parents to rubber-stamp everything the school says and does? Make bulletin boards? Sell raffle tickets? Bake cookies and cakes for bake sales? Take on decision making positions? Can parents be in a position to question a teacher about whether Columbus discovered America, or whether it's fair that some children are being ignored in a classroom and are not encouraged to participate? Only schools can determine exactly what they want parents to do.

Many times schools say they want parental involvement but when parents do begin to exert and express themselves—sometimes to the school's displeasure—the school staff is quick to remind them that they have the degrees in education, not the parents. This is not fair. I think we need to look at the position of parent coordinator in the Headstart and Chapter I programs. This person is interested in having parents involved and focuses her/his energies and skills to that end. Many of our schools have secretaries who make it very difficult for parents to even talk to a principal or teacher. At times parents feel unwanted at the school. Good principals are aware of this and realize they need a sensitive person answering the phones and greeting parents.

Q: What happened to the good old days when a child acted up and not only received discipline and chastising from his or her parents but also from the community?

A: Those good old days were based on three elements: talking and knowing each other and trust. Parents would not have felt comfortable with a neighbor spanking their child unless they trusted the neighbor. In order to trust someone you have to know the person and in order to know someone you have to talk to the person. Nowadays there are parents who have lived on a block for X number of years and do not know their neighbors. The children know the neighbors, but the parents do not.

The good old days were not based on working a 9 to 5 job, coming home and locking one or two sets of doors, and watching TV the rest of the evening. In the good old days our parents and grandparents didn't lock doors and watch television. They sat on the porch or strolled down the block and talked to each other. The more they talked, the better they understood and knew each other, and the greater trust they had in assisting each other with the development of their children. Today we no longer do that, but those days are still available to us if we will talk to each other, know each other, and ultimately trust each other.

Q: How can a single low income parent produce a high achieving student?

A: In a book titled *Family Life and School Achievement*,

Reginald Clark looks at the phenomenon of low income, high income, single parenting, and dual parenting and how these factors relate to academic achievement. He found it was not how much money or how many parents were in the home which determined academic achievement, but the quality of the interaction that took place. In high achieving homes there are five things parents do. First, they transmit *hope*. They believe the world is going to be better for their children. Conversely, in some homes the parents are downtrodden and they transmit a dismal attitude to their children. In high achieving homes parents say, "It may not be all I want it to be, but it's going to be better for my children."

Second and third, parents of high achieving children are *consistent* and *complimentary*. In some homes, Mama has one rule on Monday and another rule on Wednesday. Furthermore, in some low achieving homes, every other word has four letters and insults the children. But in high achieving homes, parents supply rules that remain unchanged from day to day, and they praise their children because they are sensitive about what they say and its effect on their offspring.

Fourth, in high achieving homes the parents give their children *high expectations*. They expect them to do well and go on to college. They give very clear messages about what's expected of them in the future. Last but not least, parents in high achieving homes believe they are the *primary educators* of their children. They do not put the major onus on the teacher. They put the major burden on themselves.

There have always been two kind of parents in America. Let's imagine them at a teacher-parent conference. The first kind of parent will respond to the teacher by passing the buck. He or she will probably say, "Well, I don't know what to do with him either. I have my own problems." Then there's the second kind of parent. This parent listens very carefully to the teacher and then says softly, "Thank you very much for telling me about my child. Now, if you can leave us alone for a moment I can assure you that you won't have any of those problems anymore." When the teacher leaves the conference she doesn't know what's going on between the parent and child. But you can imagine it's a very serious interaction, perhaps in line with what Bill Cosby told the character Theo on one of his TV programs, "I brought you in here and I'll take you out." These are the kind of parents we need more of, who take their role seriously and with complete commitment.

I like the kind of research presented by Reginald Clark. I'm not trying to sell poverty or single parenting, but it's good to know that in spite of the numbers or money in the household, parents can produce high achieving students.

Q: How do you empower parents?

A: The question is simple and complex simultaneously. On one level, we have all the power we need to do all that needs to be done for the development of our children. For example, let me ask you, do you have the ability to set goals for your children? Do you have the ability to take your children to church? Are you able to teach your children their culture and history? Can you monitor your child's peer group? Do you know your child's peer group well enough to invite them over and otherwise determine what group your child runs with? Can you monitor the television programs your child watches? Can you determine what they eat while they're at home? Are you able to have them do their chores? Can you make them go to bed at a reasonable hour? Do you have the ability to give them homework? Can you take them to the library? Are you able to visit their classrooms?

Every question I asked, parents have the ability to do. If they don't, it's only because our spirit has been broken. The chains are no longer around our wrists and ankles, they are around our minds. We have the power. The issue becomes more complex, though, because it's very difficult to empower parents who are not first empowered as adults. It's very difficult for them to be effective parents if they are not effective individuals. We must help parents realize time is their most important resource. They need to make a time chart on themselves to find out how their day is being spent.

We need to teach parents to continue to grow, develop, learn a new skill, and identify their talents. Then it will be possible for them to produce a product or provide a service that can become a means of employment and income. We need to have parents watch what they eat, exercise, and stop gossiping, cursing, and littering in our community. We need to have parents who support Black businesses and join an organization so they can more actively and productively fill their time. These are some of the ways we can empower ourselves and then empower our children.

Q: How can we improve the attendance at PTA meetings?

A: When I am invited to speak at PTA meetings I often ask principals, before the meeting starts, how many parents do they expect to be in attendance? Many times the principals say they don't know although they've sent out a thousand fliers. That tells me they know very little about Black culture. A thousand fliers may generate only 10 parents. If you want to increase attendance you may need to understand more about the culture. The oral tradition, the grapevine, a personal phone call or face-to-face invitation may be more effective methods. Secondly, if you observe the success of Headstart and Chapter I, a lot of it lies in personnel asking parents about the kind of workshops they're interested in. Many schools "teach" parents exactly the way they teach children. The school has determined what the parents should hear. Parents may not be interested in last month's minutes, budgetary changes, and personnel changes.

If we want to increase the number of parents at sessions like PTA meetings, we may need to ask them about their interests in the schools. With parents being younger and often less mature than in the past, we may need to present workshops on their own development or male/female relationships before they attend sessions on their child's development. If you want Black men to be there, you may need to offer workshops on how to find a job or how to counter the conspiracy to destroy Black boys. You may also need to provide interesting speakers. A topic might be very exciting but feature a boring speaker and this will also be a turnoff.

Gimmicks can be used to attract parents, such as providing child care, transportation, food, and a door prize, but the one which seems to be more effective is having children perform. I've been in numerous programs in which the school choir sang before I spoke, and then the principal said, "Oh, by the way, we have Dr. Jawanza Kunjufu here who will now give you a 30-minute workshop. To make sure everyone stays, the school choir will return with their closing selection after Dr. Kunjufu speaks." It's unfortunate we have to use these kinds of gimmicks, but they work and we'll have to continue using them until parents respond. Once they do attend, they can get the benefits of understanding why and how they're the primary educators.

Of course, it's very frustrating to speak to a group of ten parents when 600 were invited. But when this happens, we cannot waste the ten parents' time by talking about why the 590 other parents weren't there. Otherwise, the ten who came may not come back to the next meeting. If you give those ten parents the best workshop you can, they will spread the word to the others who didn't attend and the numbers will increase. I believe in the concept, "reach one, teach one." If you see ten parents on a particular night and they call someone else, you've seen twenty. The word will continue to grow in that way.

Q: At many meetings, whether PTA or other community groups, the same people seem to attend and the ones who need to be there seldom participate. How can we attract them?

A: I appreciate the spirit of the question and while we would all like to see more people involved in community groups, I believe the people who need to be at meetings are present because they are the leaders. If the people at a meeting will call two or three more and spread the word and those people do likewise, we will reach our goal.

We must be patient with our brothers and sisters and understand, "Wide is the gate and broad is the road that leads to destruction, and many enter through it. But small is the gate and narrow the road that leads to life, and only a few find it." William Cross' consciousness model notes five stages: pre-encounter, encounter, immersion, commitment, and internalization. Many of our people ignore or are naive about encounters with racism or obstacles to empowerment. These people remain in the pre-encounter stage. Others of us respond to crises during the encounter phase. These people attend meetings that are catastrophic in nature and approach. The majority of our people are at this stage. The third stage, immersion, requires an investment of time and energy to attend meetings, study the issues and determine responses. Amilcar Cabral said only the intellectuals will discuss and argue about ideas, the masses are concerned with basic goods and services. I witnessed this when I led a student group in college. We had few numbers, but we provided the rest of the students with a Sunday dinner not available in the dorms, kept them informed with a weekly newspaper, provided cultural entertainment, and offered tutoring to children in the neighborhood. We earned great respect because of our goods and services, not because of our ideas. There is much more I could say about this subject. The book I had planned to write, *Marketing Black Consciousness*, has these ideas and more, but the Lord told me to write *A Talk with Jawanza* and has not approved the other one.

The last two stages, commitment and internalization, have even fewer numbers. Of the ten parents who attended that PTA meeting, probably half of them are in the immersion stage — securing information. The remaining parents have moved beyond theory, have committed themselves to work, and have internalized this position without hatred or ill feelings toward anyone.

Q: I understand there's a rumor that this may be the first generation of African-American youth who will not exceed their parents in academic achievement. Can you elaborate on what you mean?

A: With every generation of African-American youth we have continued to grow in educational advancement. This may be the first generation who will not exceed their parents in academic achievement. Many of our youth have $3.00 skills and million dollar desires. There are parents who have given their children their own telephone, stereo, TV, and VCR in their room and now the children want a microwave oven. We have given our children *things* and not given them *time*.

The average father spends only seven minutes a day talking to his children and the average mother spends only 34 minutes a day talking to her children. We must realize children develop much faster and more healthily when we give them time than when we give them things. Let's make sure the rumor does not become a reality in our households.

Q: How can we improve the quality of time we spend with our children?

A: Whatever number of minutes we spend with our children need to be the best minutes of our lives. Parents need to go into their children's bedroom, sit on the bed, and simply ask them how things are going. Too many times parents talk at their children and lecture them the way teachers do; we don't listen to our youth. I believe children have a story to tell if only we will listen. If we listen well enough when our children want to talk about drugs or sex, they'll come to us rather than go to their friends. This kind of interaction affects the quality of time spent with children. I suggest parents simply be there to listen to children, play with them, and ask them what kind of games they want to play. That kind of giving not only makes you a better parent, but it also allows the child forms of expression on their level.

I think it's very helpful and effective to find out about your children's interests. The best way to do that is to simply make yourself available to them. I once had a parent tell me. "Jawanza, if you recommend at least one half hour of daily quality time and I have six children, I'm going to have to spend three hours a day with them." I told the parent thirty minutes was a suggestion and if the parent can find ways to do things collectively with her children, that's good parenting too. It's important to spend some time with your children and if it's at all possible, let some of those moments feature one-on-one quality time.

COMMUNITY INVOLVEMENT

Q: What are your feelings about Saturday and evening cultural schools?

A: I think we need one on every block. The African-American community is too dependent on schools to do so much for our children: feed them breakfast and lunch, teach them during the school day, make sure they get medical check-ups, and provide counseling and after school programs. I would like to see schools teach culture and history to our children from an African frame of reference, but we need to do this ourselves. The Jews understand that. They send their children to public schools for the three R's but they use their synagogues during after school and weekend hours to make sure their children are committed to Judaism and Israel. I repeat, we need cultural schools on every block.

In most cities there are a few after school and Saturday cultural programs for our children, but one or two schools in large cities is simply not enough. We need them in every church and community organization to make sure all of our children are receiving what I feel is a very important element in their lives, and that's our history and culture. Of course, these schools should learn from each other so we don't duplicate the wheel. There's no need, for example, for each school to develop curriculum when there are other schools that have already developed good curriculum and can inform other schools about that aspect. All the factors involved in running these kinds of schools, such as recruiting students and teachers, designing the facility, and determining the frequency of sessions, should be shared amongst the schools.

Q: What are your feelings about fulltime independent Black schools?

A: We need independent Black schools in every neighborhood. In most cities one or two exist, but we need more. The Independent Black School movement, spearheaded by the Council of Independent Black Institutions (CIBI) consists of over 40 schools. CIBI was founded in the early 1970s and is designed to fully educate our children. One problem these schools face is they're private and the children who really need the benefits of CIBI will probably never attend these schools because their parents can't afford the tuition. This same problem exists in Catholic schools which pay their teachers very low salaries because the tuition provides inadequate support—too much for needy families and too little for most teachers.

Most independent Black schools will tell you their biggest problems have been lack of finances, teacher stability, and community support. It becomes very difficult to keep a good teacher who is paid $10,000 - 15,000 a year. Commitment has its limits. I don't think we can question teachers' commitment when they point out they need medical insurance, college tuition, or money for a house. We need to find creative ways to fund these schools because they're doing an excellent job. Through activities such as their annual science fair, the kind of progress our children are making at these schools is demonstrated. Most of the independent Black schools began as preschools and many of them added a school year thereafter. Many are now complete elementary schools with grades pre-K through eight and some offer high school classes.

Q: Can you describe your Talent Center and its objectives?

A: The Talent Center is designed to identify and develop children's innate talents in nine different areas: analytical thinking, memory, oral and written communication, visual, mechanical, listening, eye-hand coordination, and concentration. So many times when we hear the word "talent," we only think of sports and music and for that reason in our community we provide 86% of the NBA's starters but only 2% of the engineers and doctors. The Talent Center is designed to expand the definition of talent beyond sports and music and encourage our children in math, science, and language arts. We attempt to develop our children's talents to expand their horizons. We also provide tutoring. Many people are using our center for remedial work and we have been able to raise test scores substantially. But we also want to be viewed as an enrichment center for students scoring above the national average. Counseling is offered for students in motivation, special education, family therapy, and career development. Ultimately, we want to have children use their talents to start their own businesses.

The Talent Center's biggest obstacle is parental support for education, not equipment, staff, facility, or curriculum. If I received a grant I would probably allocate most of it to advertising, which is disappointing. We can't expect a 12-year-old to leave the basketball court and voluntarily enroll in a science or computer class. We need parents who not only say they value education, but will take the time to enroll their child in a program of this magnitude.

Q: When adolescent females, who often times may be on drugs, give birth to children and are not effective at child rearing, live in a housing project, and do not nurture and monitor their children, what is the future for these young mothers' children?

A: This is a million dollar question and everyone wants to know the answer. We know what works best: a loving home, two parents with adequate income transmitting hope, consistency, and praise, with high expectations and a belief that they're the primary educators. But that's an unfair scenario because it describes ideal arrangements that rarely occur. We need to be honest and acknowledge our station in life is primarily because of our parents. Traditionally and historically, the group who would come to the rescue and help the particular children you describe would be the extended family, followed by schools, churches, and other community organizations.

Several factors influence the eroding network of people and services which have previously been available to adolescent mothers. One of them is that the extended family has not been as effective in recent years. Secondly, many teachers now in the schools don't look like the children they service, nor do they live in the same neighborhood. Thirdly, many churches are more attuned to prosperity than salvation. Fourth, many community organizations are overwhelmed with problems but have declining budgets. I believe the biggest issue we have to resolve concerns values. Early on, children should be taught basic values, such as politeness, cleanliness, and respect for adults, authority figures, property, and life. Those values should be taught at a very early age, and it takes time and an ongoing rapport to develop them.

When parents fail to instill these and other values, it is difficult for anyone else to do so. But life remains very simple: When we give up, we automatically lose. We must dare to struggle in order to win. There were people who thought Detroit Red was lost. His father was killed, his mother was placed in an institution, and Detroit Red went to the street and eventually prison. Elijah Muhammad was able to turn Detroit Red around. Ron Edmonds has shown that effective schools can produce high achieving students in low income areas, and I like that kind of research. As positive as my mother and father were, it was actually my track coach who turned me around. He was the one who ran us from 3:00-6:00 every evening until we were exhausted. He confirmed the idea that I was going to college and could be somebody.

It's a struggle out there between us and the streets. The peer group feels that when the home breaks down, they can be the mother and father. We have to ask ourselves if we're going to let them be the only source of direction for our children, or whether we can — as members of extended families, schools, churches, and communities — come to the rescue of these children. If we can give some direction to just one child who is not our biological child, the future will be brighter for the children you described.

AFTERWORD

When Americans felt they were losing the competitive edge to the Russians, a greater commitment to education was made. This same response has begun to emerge because of Japan's growing strength in world markets. In the African-American community we have a dropout rate in large urban areas that hovers around 50%. Forty-two percent of our youth over 17 years of age can't read beyond a sixth grade level. A 30-point differential exists between White and Black students' achievement test scores. It takes a lot to insult us. Our insult level is very high. I don't know what it will take for the larger African-American community to say these and other indications of Black youth's academic achievement are unacceptable and insulting to our race, and we now will take responsibility for our children's education or make educators do a better job. Responses from citizens in Milwaukee and Roxbury, who have proposed creating their own school district or city government, is one possible solution. Whatever methods are chosen, we can no longer afford to respond with short-term reactions to a crisis but with long-term, highly developed formats that demand excellence from our youth.

Traditionally, we have placed the education of our children in the hands of professionals. But we must be aware that a new kind of racism exists in America that's less overt but equally dangerous. Before 1954, African-American children attended school in inferior facilities with secondhand books and equipment. The only compensation for this inequitable situation was they had the best teachers in our history, ironically because of institutional racism.

Our best Black minds had limited career options and many had to teach. These teachers and their high expectations were able in most cases to offset the lack of proper resources.

The new racism allows children to attend integrated schools in better facilities, but expectations have declined. Besides the fact that many African American children still attend racially segregated schools because of housing patterns, many schools simply use tracking and special education placements to segregate schools on the inside. Curiously, many public school teachers send their own children to private or magnet schools. I believe this is the best indicator of expectations from the people who know the system best. Can you imagine what would happen if school districts required teachers to send their own children to regular public schools? I predict that if this mandate was in place, there would either be massive resignations or teachers would have to invest more effort in improving public schools because their own children would be affected. Many teachers, Black and White, who have their offspring in private and magnet schools, have placed African American children in lower tracks or special education classes, and lowered their expectations for the students they teach because they believe these "poor children" come from low income, broken homes and are culturally deprived. The few teachers who do not fit this mold, who believe African-American children can learn, are burning out and need our help.

The National Association of Black School Educators (NABSE) feels we have made enough excuses about why African-American children are not achieving academically. We need consultants who either work in effective schools or programs or have studied these strategies, or have techniques and theories that have been shown to be effective. As Asa Hilliard points out, hospitals don't bring in doctors who can't demonstrate successful surgery. Ron Edmonds has given us the theoretical background, many schools have demonstrated that his strategies work, so why are we still discussing the issue of whether African-American children can learn? The Council of Independent Black Institutions has shown culture and identity enhance self-esteem and academic achievement. SETCLAE has a model that can be used in the school setting; why are we still discussing why African-American children can't learn? We know that Headstart and Chapter I are effective and that parents can be empowered through these programs as well as through methods based on the research from Reginald Clark and James Comer—why are we saying that intervention and parental involvement can't be achieved? We know that cooperative learning works, both in elementary and high school, and it can be used to overcome problems college students experience with courses like calculus and statistics. So why aren't we using it more often? In just one year of our Talent Center's operation, I have observed a marked increase in test scores simply because, like Asians, we increased students' study time qualitatively. I've also observed that our Black male classroom and rites of passage programs have provided major sources of direction to African-American boys who once were lost. Why have't we instituted more programs like these?

We know the problems and their causes. With our limited time and money we must now talk only about solutions and their implementation.

PLEDGE ON BLACK MANHOOD

I am the Black man
Some know me as Imhotep, Ramses,
        Martin or Malcolm.
Others know me as the brother on the corner
        or in jail.

I am both, Detroit Red and Malcolm.
From this day forward, I pledge my life
        to the liberation of my people.
I will put God first in my life.
Black women will feel safe when they see me.
I will be a supportive, responsible,
        and loving husband.
I will hug, talk and listen to, and
        educate my children.
I will be involved in the Scouts,
Role Model and Rites-of-Passage.

Why?
Because I am the Black man — the original man,
        the one and only.
The one that other men are afraid of,
        because they know whenever
        I've been given the opportunity — I succeed.

JAWANZA KUNJUFU